COUNTRY INNS
OF NEW YORK STATE

OTHER BOOKS IN THE COUNTRY INNS SERIES

COUNTRY INNS
OF NEW YORK STATE

ROBERT W. TOLF
ROXANE S. RAUCH

ROY KILLEEN
Illustrations

101 PRODUCTIONS
San Francisco

COVER DRAWING: Asa Ransom House, Clarence, New York. Drawing by Roy Killeen, color rendering by Sara Raffetto.

MAPS: Lynne O'Neil

Some of the drawings in this book have been reproduced from the inns' brochures with the permission of the inns, and are credited to the following artists: The Country Inn, page 6, David Hutchinson; Village Latch Inn, page 9, Jan Bradt; Huntting Inn, page 12, Madelleyn; Shepherds Neck Inn, page 18, Palagomia; Chequit Inn, page 21, R. M. Webb; Ram's Head Inn, page 23; The Algonquin, page 30; The Box Tree, page 38; The Bird & Bottle Inn, page 39, James Detlifs; Hudson House, page 43, James Detlifs; One Market Street, page 44, James Detlifs; Cottonwood Inn, page 48, Robert Palmer; L'Hostellerie Bressane, page 52; Millhof Inn, page 57, Len Marshick; Astoria Hotel, page 63, Arthur Gleissner; Baker's, page 67, Frances A. Sutherland; Redcoat's Return, page 73, Susan Yule; Winter Clove Inn, page 75, Linda Boutin; Trout House Village, page 97, Emily Sola; The Hedges, page 104, Jean Wilson; Mirror Lake Inn, page 110, Dan Ferguson; Stagecoach Inn, page 112, Peter Moreau; The Bark Eater, page 114; The Inn at Brook Willow Farm, page 119; Worthington House, page 122, Anna Roemer; Lincklaen House, page 132; The Cecce House, page 145, Eunice Nesbit; Rosewood Inn, page 146, Joyce M. Snyder; Rose Inn, page 148, Elinor Hawkins; Sherwood Inn, page 155; the Inn at Belhurst Castle, page 162; Avon Inn, page 164, Lisa Forster; Genesee Falls Inn, page 169; William Seward Inn, page 175, Wm. Larrymore Smedley; Leland House, page 177, Randall Arumn.

Printed and bound in the United States of America. Distributed to the book trade in the United States by The Scribner Book Companies, New York, and in Canada by John Wiley & Sons Canada, Limited, Toronto.

Published by 101 Productions
834 Mission Street, San Francisco, California 94103

Library of Congress Cataloging in Publication Data

Tolf, Robert W.
  Country inns of New York State.

  Includes index.
  1. Hotels, taverns, etc.—New York (State)—Directories.
I. Title.
TX907.T5328   1984   647'.9474701   84–13171
ISBN 0–89286–233–5

CONTENTS

We dedicate this book to Carolyn, David, and Janine—and all the tasteful adventurers of this world who are not "too late smart."

INTRODUCTION

In the beginning this book was going to be a guide to the country inns of all the Mid-Atlantic states, but as the riches of New York unfolded, with one wonderful inn after another surrounded by a multitude of marvelous attractions, natural and manmade, it became obvious that New York must stand on its own.

Country inns are definitely In. They are soothing escapes and blessed retreats blending yesterday and today into a strong affirmation of our past and guaranteeing survival into the future.

A colorful quilt, a hand-carved curving staircase, the smell of fresh-baked bread, an open hearth—an inn exudes a warmth that gives one a sense of belonging. It transforms lackluster comfort into a gracious level of taste that is ever so seductive.

Along with the comforts, the amenities, the sense of place encountered in visiting these inns came the repeated pleasure of learning that so very many of New York's inns are concentrating on their kitchens, offering guests well-bred fare starting with breakfasts built around a bounty of yummy breads and muffins, luscious home-potted preserves, even eggs and maple syrup from their own farms. Dinners, lunches, and brunches have more in common with the sophisticated palates of the city than with the often-casual cooking encountered on the back roads of the countryside.

It was a joyous journey, criss-crossing the state again and again to visit each and every inn in the book (and a good many which are not), determining which passed muster for inclusion. Personal reconnaissance, on-the-scene surveys and inspections, sometimes with the knowledge of the owners and operators, often without, were the prerequisites for determining whether or not an inn should be included in this book.

There is no innkeepers' association to join, no requirements to sell this book, no fees requested or required of the inns featured here. That kind of boodle represents as great a disservice to the reader, and the inn-goer, as guides that base their judgment merely on responses to questionnaires, on whatever a given innkeeper chooses to report.

It's far more expensive, in time and treasure, to visit all the real estate, to pay for all those meals and all the accommodations, but it's the only honest route to writing this kind of book.

What kind of inn made the final cut? What Webster defines as "a public house for the lodging and entertainment of travelers or wayfarers for a compensation," with our own "inn-ovative" definition: an experience apart, an exposure to something special, no matter the size or cost.

We sought instant removal from the doldrums of Samesville, USA, and innkeepers who really cared about the comforts of their guests and were willing to take the extra steps to make their inn the very best, to bring to life the words of Samuel Johnson: "There is nothing which has yet been contrived by man by which so much happiness is produced as by a good tavern or inn."

We honor those innkeepers who made our task of research so very, very enjoyable. They are making American hospitality come of age.

RULES OF THE INN

Reservations, Deposits, and Rates   Reservations are required for most of the inns and should be made as far in advance as possible, especially during peak travel times. Many inns require an advance deposit, an amount which may vary as much as the basic room rates. For obvious reasons specific rates are not quoted. Inexpensive means just that: less than an average motel room in the area. Expensive is equivalent to the tariff in a first-class hotel; very expensive equal to a super-luxe hotel. Moderate is somewhere in between.

Housekeeping   In the smaller inns with shared baths the guest is responsible for cleaning the sink and tub. The rooms, often cleaned by the innkeeper doubling as chambermaid, should be kept in good order.

Tipping   In the smaller places, discuss it with the innkeeper; many might be embarrassed by a gratuity or insulted by the offer but would welcome a thank-you note or the kind of bread-and-butter gift you would send if staying at someone's home.

LONG ISLAND
NEW YORK CITY

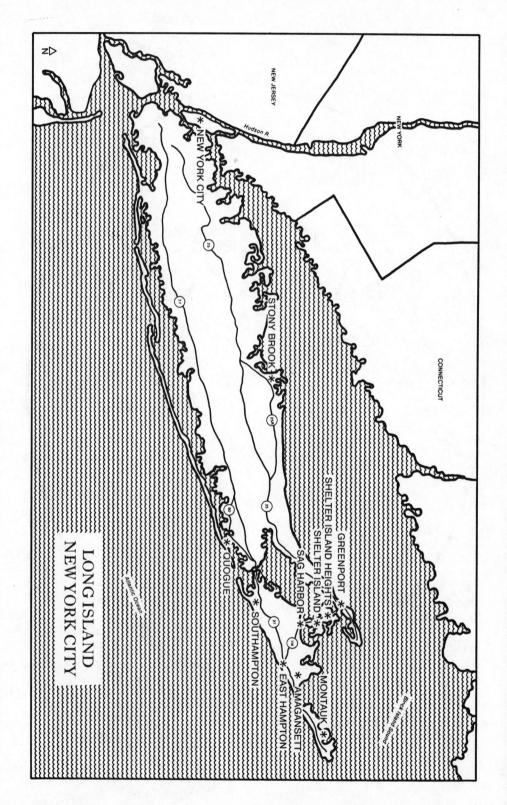

LONG ISLAND
NEW YORK CITY

N

NEW JERSEY

NEW YORK

CONNECTICUT

Hudson R

NEW YORK CITY

STONY BROOK

Atlantic Ocean

CUTCHOGUE

SOUTHAMPTON

EAST HAMPTON

AMAGANSETT

SAG HARBOR

SHELTER ISLAND HEIGHTS
SHELTER ISLAND

GREENPORT

MONTAUK

Block Island Sound

LONG ISLAND

Three Stars for Starr

THE INN AT QUOGUE

Quogue

Between the bays named Quantuck and Shinnecock, beautifully dominating a corner of what is officially known as the Quogues, this classic inn has one of the best kitchens in the state. The resident super chef is Starr Boggs, a bear of a man who got most of his on-the-job training at the Williamsburg Inn in his native Virginia; but he also cooked up a storm in Palm Beach for a time (at Le Café and Truffles), and in nearby Westhampton he's in charge of the back room at the Patio on Main Street, a handsomely appointed retreat owned and operated by the master of the Inn at Quogue, Susan Mc-Allister.

The energetic, entrepreneurial Susan is one of the five women who banded together in Westhampton a few years ago to open Manhattan's excellent Summerhouse restaurant, and she spends at least a month each winter in Palm Beach. That's where she recruits staff members such as inn-keeper/manager Brian Moorhead, who's in charge of the appealing lounge, where there's usually a crackling fire.

Starr is the resident expert on the wines of the area, especially the vintages of Alex and Louise Hargrave. The Pinot Noir from their Long Island winery is a noble companion to Starr's exciting creations: chilled red pepper soup; purée of black beans with crème fraîche and chopped scallions; a spicy fish brew; fresh-caught fluke bathed in a memorable herb butter sprinkled with cracked pepper and lightly sautéed gooseberries; sea scallops in a garlic-mustard sauce; puréed carrots with a hint of turnip; sautéed squash showered with chopped fresh basil. And for desserts, try orange slices marinated in Grand Marnier; praline cheese cake christened

3

The Inn at Quogue

with a sauce tasting of espresso; a triple-tier cake that's a chocoholic's delight.

The baker's dozen collection of guest rooms are not as exciting as the creations of Starr's kitchen, but there are a few antiques here and there, a pair of comfortably furnished suites on the ground floor, and upstairs rooms decorated in the sweet dreams of the "girl next door."

And there is definitely a sense of history. The inn is close to two centuries old. It was known for years as the Hallock House, and for many years was owned and operated by the same couple who ran Nando's in Palm Beach. But it's hard to believe it's ever been better than under the McAllister-Boggs regime. Check in for a night or longer and work through that menu, or check in for a dinner in the strikingly understated dining room with its many windows, attractive bentwood chairs, and glass table covers over cheerful chintz.

THE INN AT QUOGUE, Quogue Street, Quogue, New York 11959. Telephone: (516) 653-6560. Accommodations: 13 rooms, 11 with private bath; no televisions or telephones. Rates: expensive; includes breakfast. Cards: AE, MC, V. Inquire about children; no pets. Open mid-May through mid-September.

Getting There: The inn is in the center of Quogue, at the corner of Quogue Street and Jessup Avenue.

From Cottage to Country Inn
THE COUNTRY INN
Southampton

John Daniele and Garry Jackson worked the wonder of restoration and revitalization on this one-time summer cottage whose foundations go back some two hundred years. In 1982 the task of transformation was complete, and the tall frame structure nestled in a grove of towering trees was finished off in great style.

Antiques are placed here and there, not in profusion, but with a sparing touch, blending with the light earth tones of peach, brown, white, beige and tan. The trim inside and out is impeccable, the level of maintenance faultless, and, out back, occupying center stage of a rolling expanse of lawn, is a swimming pool and a gazebo. The front of the inn has a comfortable porch for taking in the quieter side of Southampton.

For some of the excitement, from horse shows to restored mansions, check with the very well organized Chamber of Commerce Visitor Center in town at 76 Main Street. En route, do a bit of window shopping or search for stylish finds on Job's Lane—Saks, Elizabeth Arden, Shep Miller, Ann Taylor, Lilly Pulitzer, and Kassatly's are all there.

Southampton, as the visitor soon learns, is where a lot of old wealth resides. Westhampton has been compared to the high-tech energy of south Florida and California, and Bridgehampton and East Hampton are, of course, where the writers and artists flee for summer R and R—except for those who find greater privacy out on the point in Montauk and the lesser towns that dot the South Fork.

John Daniele can fill in the details while explaining where he got the idea of becoming an innkeeper, and where he got the inspiration for those two marvelous rooms, the Gable in front and the Tower Room behind it.

THE COUNTRY INN, 200 Hill Street, Southampton, New York 11968. Telephone: (516) 283-4849. Accommodations: 10 rooms; no televisions or telephones. Rates: moderate; includes Continental breakfast. Cards: AE. Pets not permitted. Open May through October.

Getting There: The inn is on the same street as the Hill Guest House, across the street and closer to the center of Southampton.

6

Italian Hospitality
HILL GUEST HOUSE
Southampton

Mauro and Ronnie Salerno have been running this happily maintained but unadorned five-room guest house for a couple of decades. With all the verve and the vigor of dedicated innkeepers, they serve Continental breakfasts to guests—for a minimal extra charge—and guide them to the sights and sites of Southampton. Mauro knows the Hamptons and keeps track of all the changes in the area.

The Salernos, who keep a very neat house indeed, will also instruct their guests about the best driving tours of the area, from Halsey Neck Lane to the dunes and all the great oceanfront estates on Meadow Lane.

The Salernos, whose parents came from southern Italy, can deliver their suggestions in Italian, or, in the case of wife Ronnie, in French. Each winter, during their off season, they go back to the old country to relax and recuperate from their labors as conscientious innkeepers.

HILL GUEST HOUSE, 535 Hill Street, Southampton, Long Island, New York 11968. Telephone: (516) 283-9889. Winter address: 43–35 169th Street, Flushing, New York 11358; telephone: (212) 461-0014. Accommodations: six rooms, two sharing a bath; no televisions or telephones. Rates: inexpensive to low moderate. Continental breakfast served for slight charge. No cards. Pets not permitted. Open May 1 to November 1.

Getting There: Hill Street is also State Route 27A, Montauk Highway; the inn is on the left side of the street coming the two miles on 27A from Exit 7 of Route 27.

English Tudor Excellence
SOUTHAMPTON INN
Southampton

For serious shoppers visiting Southampton, this is the place to stay. Opened in the early 1970s and looking like an English inn Tudor style, it's only minutes from the stores on Job's Lane in the center of the village, and right across a wide expanse of lawn and well-manicured gardens from the International Plaza with still more shopping.

The inn rooms are individually decorated and modern, and there's a liberal use of brightly colored bedspreads, drapes, wall coverings. Favorite rooms here overlook the pool and the lushest part of the landscaping.

There are on- and off-season package rates, including intensive tennis instruction and golfing in the Hamptons—enough activity to make the inn's sauna and Jacuzzi most welcome after a day of exertion. On the lighter side, the inn is the home of the East End Comedy Club, the comedy showcase of the Hamptons.

SOUTHAMPTON INN, Southampton, Long Island, New York 11968. Telephone: (516) 283-6500. Accommodations: 90 rooms, each with private bath, television, and telephone. Rates: expensive. Cards: AE, CB, DC, MC, V. No pets permitted. Open all year.

Getting There: The inn is a few hundred yards west of the center of the village.

A Theatrical Resort

VILLAGE LATCH INN
Southampton

Innkeepers Marta and Martin White are a unique asset in the Hamptons, where they have created a five-acre resort just a block from the special shops on Job's Lane. A theatrical producer and director, and a high-spirited woman with an intense gaze, Marta is an indefatigable gatherer of the world's old goods. She has amassed an incredible assortment of antiques and artifacts, filling her ramble of rooms with more reminders of the past than most antique dealers can claim.

In her television room, the least interesting item is the set itself. Everything else is fascinating, guaranteed to provoke comment if not lengthy conversation. An adjoining room is all wicker, and across a little lobby filled with you-name-it-it's-there is the breakfast room, a do-it-yourself affair with a bin of bagels, ingredients for omelets, pots and pots of coffee and tea, and a general sense of camaraderie among guests eager to share their experiences in and out of the Hamptons.

Those rooms are in the main structure, the one-time annex to Southampton's famous Irving Hotel, oldest hostelry on Eastern Long Island. It would now be just a memory were it not for the Whites, who imported other

buildings for their five acres and then added a swimming pool, a pitch-and-putt course, a tennis court, and a small gazebo as a shady retreat.

There is much here to appeal to guests, many hiding places to discover behind all those French doors and oversize windows—including a hot tub in a Victorian greenhouse—that Marta and Martin's creation is one of the highlights of the Hamptons.

VILLAGE LATCH INN, 101 Hill Street, Southampton, New York 11968. Telephone: (516) 283-2160. Accommodations: 45 rooms, most with private bath; some televisions or telephones. Rates: moderate; includes full breakfast. Cards: AE, MC, V. Children not permitted; no pets. Open year round.

Getting There: The inn is across from the Southampton Inn.

A New England Import
BASSETT HOUSE
East Hampton

Innkeeper Mike Bassett is a native of Braintree, Massachusetts, and a lover of the country inns of New England. And that's what he's managed to create across the border in his adopted Hamptons: a touch of Vermont and Massachusetts in this suburbia-by-the-sea.

Private and public rooms are filled with what he's found in the famous yard sales of the Hamptons and what he's bought at auction. Mike is not a fussy collector; he's filled with a sense of fun and is constantly working on his pride and joy.

9

In room Number 5 there's a magnificent spindle bed made of solid oak, and in room Number 1 is another antique bed along with a splendid old rug, walk-in closets, a large bathroom, corner windows, and interesting accent pieces.

Some of the rooms have fireplaces, and for those Mike charges more in the off-season than during the summer months when the Hamptons swarm with what sometimes seems like just about everybody from the big city.

BASSETT HOUSE, 128 Montauk Highway (P.O. Box 1426), East Hampton, New York 11937. Telephone: (516) 324-6127. Accommodations: 12 rooms, three with private bath, seven with shared baths; no televisions or telephones in rooms; television in living room. Rates: moderate to expensive; includes full breakfast. Cards: AE, MC, V. Pets permitted for extra charge. Open all year except for several weeks during January and February.

Getting There: Montauk Highway is State Road 27, and the inn is 1.5 miles west of the village of East Hampton.

A Colonial Charmer

HEDGES HOUSE
East Hampton

The first Hedges inn was established during the Great Depression, in a grand old three-story survivor of the American Revolution. During the 1950s, Henri Soule of Manhattan's famed Le Pavillon ran it as a summer mission to the provinces. In 1979 the present owners, Kenneth Baker and Richard Spencer, took over, and after an extensive period of renovation and restoration reopened Hedges House in June 1981.

It's hard to believe that the historic home—listed on the National Register—has ever been better. The outdoor terrace is surrounded by carefully tended gardens, the interior dining rooms are charmingly Colonial, and the guest rooms upstairs are color coordinated, with linens and bedspreads accented by period pieces that add mightily to the feeling that one is in a country inn of considerable class.

Room Number 1, with its double bed, is in the front of the house. It has a fireplace and a fine view of the street leading into what the owners here regard as "America's most beautiful village." Room Number 10, with its king-size bed, also has a fireplace. Third-floor attic rooms are preferred by some guests because of their odd configurations and their gables.

The restaurant is known as En Brochette; that's also the name of the owner's restaurant in Beverly Hills. The menu has entrées of chicken, duckling, and jalapeño beef en brochette. The kitchen concentrates on freshness, on relatively few sauces, and light seasoning. As Baker and Spencer explain on their menu: "We have great concern for perfection and quality, but most of all there is a sense of humor as rules are broken and inventiveness reigns." It is their ardent desire to create "flavors that are fresh, clear and distinct."

To the left it's a 10-minute walk to the beach. To the right, walk along James Lane to the Home Sweet Home Museum, a saltbox that is one of the two oldest houses in the village. Built in 1750, it was the home of John Howard Payne, who wrote "Home Sweet Home" while living in Paris in the 1820s and longing for East Hampton.

HEDGES HOUSE, 74 James Lane, East Hampton, New York 11937. Telephone: (516) 324-7100. Accommodations: 14 rooms, each with private bath, some with fireplaces; no televisions or telephones. Rates: expensive. Cards: AE, MC, V. Pets not permitted. Open all year.

Getting There: The inn is across from the town pond just off State Road 27.

Palm in the Provinces
HUNTTING INN
East Hampton

If you are familiar with the Palm Restaurant in New York City, you'll have no hesitancy about checking into this beautifully landscaped landmark that has been a "Publick House" for two centuries. Those Palm purveyors of king-sized steaks and giant-sized lobsters are in charge of this building, which has origins going all the way back to 1699. During the American Revolution, it was the only place on the South Fork where Colonial and British combatants could meet under flags of truce.

In recent years Palm has become a familiar name to steak and lobster lovers in other areas as the owners have aggressively expanded into other markets in Miami Beach, Chicago, and as far afield as California. But only in the Hamptons have they added overnight lodging to their portfolio.

The guest rooms are not elaborate, but they provide a general atmosphere of country comfort with functional furnishings, a selection of brass beds covered with quilts and ruffles, and a chocolate placed on each pillow nightly.

HUNTTING INN, 94 Main Street, East Hampton, New York 11937. Telephone: (516) 324-0410. Accommodations: 26 rooms, 22 with private bath; telephones but no televisions. Rates: moderate. Full bar and meal service. Cards: AE, CB, DC, MC, V. Pets not permitted. Open April to December.

Getting There: The inn is on the corner of Main Street and Huntting Lane, next to the Presbyterian Church.

Culinary Champion

THE MAIDSTONE ARMS
East Hampton

The food in this inn, thanks to chef Morris Weintraub, is probably on a par with that served at the 1770 House down the street. And that's quite a par to be on. Weintraub's veal piccata Prince Orlof with a veal glaze and mushroom purée is fit for a king, and his Long Island duckling, capon française, poached fish Duglère, and seafood on a bed of rice pilaf are superlative. So is the wine list.

This fine fare is served in a classic country inn setting nestled in the trees across from the Village Green and the Town Pond, in the heart of the National Historic District. The original section, the main house, dates from 1750. Two centuries later, after the Civil War, what had been a private home was converted into a hotel.

The guest rooms are furnished with period pieces to help capture the past, and the wicker-filled sun porch, where guests gather each morning for the complimentary Continental breakfast, is straight from the Victorian era. But the books and magazines are more contemporary and are in constant circulation among those who want to rest after all the excitement of the Hamptons.

The inn is ideally located for those who want to stroll the streets of one of the state's most beautiful settlements, founded in 1649. For a self-guided map to the old mills and burying grounds and the historic houses of special interest, check into the Chamber of Commerce at 74 Park Place.

THE MAIDSTONE ARMS, 207 Main Street, East Hampton, New York 11937. Telephone: (516) 324-5006. Accommodations: 18 rooms, including three 2-room suites and two cottages, each with private bath; no televisions; telephones. Rates: moderate to expensive; includes Continental breakfast. Cards: AE, MC, V. Pets not permitted. Open all year.

Getting There: The inn is on the main street of the village, State Road 27.

A Gem of the Perles

1770 HOUSE
East Hampton

Miriam ("Mim") Perle is the super chef who brings such great distinction to this historic home; her husband, Sid, acts as front man, but he's really more of a curator.

The building they bought in 1977 is now a mini-museum filled with a grand variety of antiques and such unique artifacts as a wall and windows from the town's first post office. In room Number 4, next to the canopy bed—the kind found in the other rooms—there's a night stand made out of an old glass candy display stand with a lovely doll inside.

There are antique clocks everywhere, old advertisements artfully arranged, and exposed-brick walls. The old library has pecan paneling and a fireplace, one of many in a house that has served many masters, including the Clinton Academy next door. Built in 1784, it was the first chartered secondary school in the state and is now operated by the East Hampton Historical Society.

The 1770 House used to be the dining room for the boys of the Academy, but they could not have eaten as well as present-day guests. Dinners are always *prix fixe* and are always imaginative. A sample menu might include starters of cappellini al pesto, or lobster in an orange-thyme dressing,

13

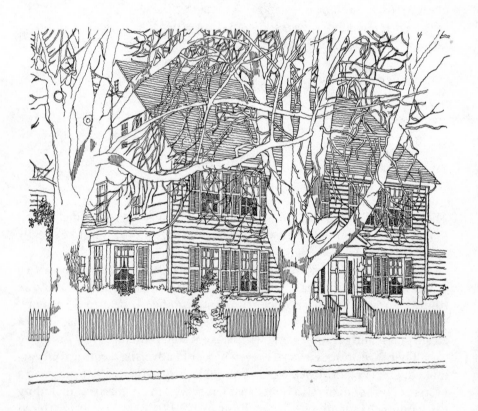

1770 House

or chilled poached salmon in a sour cream–dill dressing, followed by entrées of crispy roast duckling with lingonberry glaze; chicken dijonnaise; shrimp-crab Creole; and desserts of old-fashioned blueberry crisp or peach Melba.

1770 HOUSE, 143 Main Street, East Hampton, New York 11937. Telephone: (516) 324-1770. Accommodations: seven rooms, each with private bath; no televisions or telephones. Rates: moderate. No cards. Children under 12 not permitted; no pets. Open all year except for a few weeks in the winter.

Getting There: The inn is in the center of the village across from Guild Hall.

A Pastoral Paradise
GANSETT GREEN MANOR
Amagansett

If you're searching in the Hamptons for the idyllic little pastoral hideaway, one so farmyard rustic that there are even sheep to pet, then go no further than the Gansett Green Manor, "The Little Hampton," as its owners call their bucolic retreat, an unassuming oasis of tranquility in all the Hampton excitement.

The main house up front has guest rooms, studio efficiencies, and one- and two-bedroom suites. The cottages and apartments come complete with fireplaces and garden terraces. There are also kitchens in the larger units, and that makes them ideal for a family interested in establishing a beachhead while enjoying all there is to do in the Hamptons—on and off the water.

High season in the Hamptons is after May 20 and before September 12, and, typically for the area, room rates drop 30 percent in the off season.

GANSETT GREEN MANOR, Main Street (P.O. Box 799), Amagansett, New York 11930. Telephone: (516) 267-3133. Accommodations: 19 rooms, suites, and cottages, some sharing baths; each with television; no telephones. Rates: inexpensive to moderate. Cards: MC, V. No pets. Open May 1 to November 1.

Getting There: The manor is in the center of the village on Main Street (State Road 27), across the street from St. Peter's Church.

Resort Residences
THE MILL-GARTH
Amagansett

Three miles east of East Hampton and a dozen west of Montauk Point, the tip of Long Island, the quiet little village of Amagansett sometimes seems to be still undiscovered. In the heart of what a metropolitan would consider semi-isolation, there's the Mill-Garth complex of well-tended gardens, sweeping lawns, shaded groves, scattered statuary, and private residences furnished with considerable attention to comfort and taste.

The seven apartment units and the quartet of cottages provide perfect nesting places for couples wanting to escape and families eager to establish a home away from home. The Ivy Suite has a spacious living room with a queen-size canopy bed, a sitting room and patio, a full kitchen with skylight. The Grapevine, on the second floor of the main building, a century-old farmhouse, has an outdoor dining balcony; the Willows is on the ground floor and has three walls of windows; the Gazebo is octagonal-shaped and has a flagstone terrace out front.

The Carriage House is probably the most popular accommodation at the Mill-Garth. Its peaked ceiling of exposed beams covers twenty-two square feet of living room with a fireplace; there are two bedrooms, a large kitchen, two bathrooms, and a private patio.

Just up the road from this idyllic retreat—on a street with the happy name of Windmill Lane—there's Miss Amelia's Cottage, an early eighteenth-century home operated by the Amagansett Historical Society. On Bluff Road in town there's the Marine Museum maintained by the East Hampton Historical Society. With its underwater archeological display, its several models of fishing boats and its many exhibits of the fishing and whaling industry from earliest times, the museum is worth a special trip.

THE MILL-GARTH, Windmill Lane, Amagansett, New York 11930. Telephone: (516) 267-3757. Accommodations: seven apartments and four cottages, each with private bath, kitchen, or kitchenette; some with television; no telephones. Rates: expensive. No cards. No pets permitted. Open all year.

Getting There: Follow State Road 27, the Sunrise Highway, through Southampton and East Hampton and in Amagansett turn left at the Mobil Station (the first left after the Bayberry Nursery) onto Windmill Lane and to the inn on the left.

Budget-Pleaser

HEWITT'S RUSCHMEYER'S INN
Montauk

It's a little untrimmed around the edges, but the grounds are spacious and the atmosphere is vintage family outing, 1940s style. There's a swimming pool and rowboats for fresh-water fishing, and while the younger set is off riding ponies, parents can be preparing the barbecue alongside picnic tables shaded by a grove of trees.

The row of rooms are motel-simple in furnishings—and priced accordingly—and some share baths; but the restaurant on the premises is reliable, and equally pleasing to the budget.

Included in the almost endless array of appetizers and entrées are such favorites as steamers served in their own broth with drawn butter, mussels in white wine and garlic, clams Posilipo, all kinds of flounder and shrimp/scallop combinations, seafood Savannah or Stroganoff, and cioppino.

The owners here also operate the Shagwong Restaurant on Main Street in Montauk and can thus take advantage of greater volume when ordering provisions than most country inns with considerably more modest restaurant proportions.

HEWITT'S RUSCHMEYER'S INN, Second House Road, Montauk, New York 11954. Telephone: (516) 668-2877. Accommodations: 15 rooms, some with shared bath; televisions but no telephones. Rates: inexpensive to low moderate. Cards: AE, MC, V. Pets permitted. Open May 1 to November 1.

Getting There: From Hither Hills Highway west of Montauk turn left at Second House Road and follow it to the inn on Fort Pond Lake.

A Country Inn by the Sea

SHEPHERD'S NECK INN
Montauk

Marie and George Hammer are in charge of this country inn by the sea. Since Shepherd's Neck greeted its first guest in 1976, the Hammers have poured the profits back into their labor of love, most recently adding a wide wooden deck and staircase to the back of the second-floor guest rooms and expanding and remodeling the dining room and lounge along with the poolside outdoor cafe.

The menu was expanded in 1984, reflecting the presence of both an Italian and Greek chef (with another chef in charge of the breakfasts), and it's changed daily to keep the modified American plan guests from getting bored. Shell steak and 1½-pound Montauk lobsters are regular entrées. They might be joined by duckling à l'orange or half a broiled chicken, soft-shell crabs or a special version of shrimp scampi, then some moussaka and pastitsio, with old-fashioned rice pudding for dessert.

The setting is not sophisticated, nor are the functionally furnished rooms in the super-luxe category. But the prices are right, and in addition to the swimming pool there are nightly movies, basketball, tennis, shuffleboard and volleyball courts, and an area for barbecuing, and the ocean is only a few seconds away.

SHEPHERD'S NECK INN, Second House Road, Montauk Point, New York 11954. Telephone: (516) 668-2105. Accommodations: 65 rooms, each with private bath and color television; no telephones. Rates: inexpensive to moderate; bed and breakfast and modified American plan available. Cards: AE, CB, DC, MC, V. Pets not permitted. Open May 1 to November 1.

Getting There: The inn is on Second House Road, marked with a sign, off State Road 27 before Montauk Village; follow Second House Road three blocks to the inn.

Neat as the Proverbial Pin

WINDJAMMER
Montauk

Not far from the sandy beaches of Montauk, out where Rudolph Valentino shot his desert films and where Teddy Roosevelt took his Rough Riders to recover from the rigors of the charge up that famous hill, Socrates and Tricia Hiotakis have established an extremely well maintained inn.

Guest rooms are motel modern, and they adjoin the Windjammer restaurant, with a menu noon and night that shows off Socrates's background and talents—spanakopeta, pastitsio, moussaka, shrimp saganaki, dolmades, along with a traditional Greek salad. And there are such solid standbys as roast Long Island duckling, chops and steaks, lobster Newberg, coq au vin, and Socrates's version of paella.

The building was constructed after the disastrous hurricane of 1938 devastated the area and the previous structure on the site. When the Hiotakises took over, they thoroughly modernized the restaurant and the rooms that are spread out on two floors. The top deck has all queen-size beds; below are all doubles.

The Windjammer, out near the point of land jutting into the Atlantic, is a welcome hideaway that maintains the sense of privacy that is increasingly difficult to find amid all the hustle and hype of the Hamptons.

WINDJAMMER, Edgemere Street (P.O. Box U), Montauk, New York 11954. Telephone: (516) 668-2872. Accommodations: 18 rooms, each with private bath and television; no telephones. Rates: moderate. Cards: AE, MC, V. Pets not permitted. Open March through December.

Getting There: From Montauk Highway east of town take Edgemere Street to the inn on Fort Pond Lake.

Yankee Doodle Dining with a French Accent

THE AMERICAN HOTEL
Sag Harbor

Smack in the center of this bustling-in-the-summer, sleepy-in-the-winter one-time whaling center is the best restaurant in the area, located on the ground floor of the most historic hostelry in the area. It was built in 1846 and taken over by its present owners a dozen years ago. You'll know it when you see it—it's not a whale of an antique, just a genuine little one.

The rooms are not elaborate but they do provide a comfortable retreat after a day of exploring the countryside and waterfront. Room 12 has a skylight and 15 a large double bed and more space than the other rooms.

The kitchen and dining room are really what make this landmark something to write home about. On our last swing through Sag Harbor the back room was of course serving Long Island oysters and lobster, but the duckling was imported from Wisconsin. Their weakfish, served meunière or amadine, was from local waters as was the bluefish, prepared in a fine Roquefort sauce. Sea scallops are blessed with Pernod, the chicken with tarragon. Tournedos Rossini, a classic dish of the French repertoire, is usually on the menu, along with chateaubriand printanière and rack of lamb "aux herbes de Provence." The wine cellar is considered to be among the best in the country.

Not far distant from the American Hotel is the Sag Harbor Whaling Museum, on the corner of Main and Garden streets (open May 15–September 30). Once the home of Benjamin Huntting, owner of a fleet of whaling ships, and built the year before the hotel, it's a "must stop" for all those interested in the history of the town and its once all-important whaling industry.

THE AMERICAN HOTEL, Main Street, Sag Harbor, New York 11963. Telephone: (516) 725-3535. Accommodations: eight rooms, each with private bath; no televisions or telephones. Rates: inexpensive to moderate. No cards. No pets permitted. Open all year.

Getting There: The hotel is in the center of town, on its main street.

A Clapboard Memory Bank

CHEQUIT INN
Shelter Island

If ever an inn could be characterized as a classic nineteenth-century seashore inn, it's the Chequit, climbing up a hillside of this special island strategically situated between Orient and Montauk points.

Opened as an inn in 1871, the Chequit is a storehouse of memories of a slower-paced era.

In the lobby is a grand brass chandelier from the old Montauk Yacht Club; in the dining room is a mantelpiece that once belonged to William Randolph Hearst; the guest rooms are a hodge-podge of furnishings collected over the decades by a procession of innkeepers. And everywhere there's the feeling that this was here when your grandmother was in her prime—no, your great-grandmother.

The patio-terrace out front and the wraparound porch are great for absorbing the laid-back mellowness of the island, and the dining room serves the kind of reliable freshness one would hope to find so close to the water. The menu, featuring Long Island duckling along with the catch of the day, is changed daily, but there are regular entrées, such as clam chowder, that are always available, with specials on certain days of the week.

An annex, the Cedar Lodge, is a bit more modern in mood, but nowhere in the Chequit should one expect to find anything luxurious or new.

CHEQUIT INN, 23 Grand Avenue, Shelter Island, New York 11965. Telephone: (516) 749-0018. Accommodations: 44 rooms, each with private bath; no televisions or telephones. Rates: moderate; modified American plan available. Cards: AE, CB, DC, MC, V. Pets not permitted. Open May 1 to October 1.

Getting There: Grand Avenue is Route 114, which leads directly from the Greenport Ferry dock.

A Beachfront Resort

THE PRIDWIN

Shelter Island

Dominating a corner of Crescent Beach, overlooking the waters of the bay leading back to the northern prong of Long Island, the Pridwin is a classic country summer resort with rooms in the main building as well as cottages (some with fireplaces). The dining rooms overlook the water, there's a grandly spacious porch facing the same direction, and on warm summer evenings there are outdoor buffets and cookouts.

That second-floor deck is also the rallying point for the nightly ritual of sunset watching. During the day the myriad activities oriented to the water are on view, and that means sailing, water skiing, paddle-boating, and of course swimming, all from the Pridwin's private dock and gently sloping private beach.

Also on the premises are tennis, badminton and shuffleboard courts, and places for pitching horseshoes, playing croquet or Ping-Pong, and all kinds of indoor games to amuse the younger set.

During the season, July 1–Labor Day, accommodations are strictly modified American plan (breakfast and dinner) and at other times European plan, with a complimentary Continental breakfast served during early summer and early fall weekends. Before May 27 and after October 10 maid service is not provided unless specifically requested.

The common rooms are full of wicker, and there are fireplaces for cooler days and nights. Guest rooms are furnished in a modernized rustic style. For those wishing housekeeping facilities, there are the cottages tucked among the trees of this island the locals sometimes call "The Bermuda of the North."

THE PRIDWIN, Crescent Beach (P.O. Box J), Shelter Island, New York 11964. Telephone: (516) 749-0476. Accommodations: 40 rooms and eight cottages, each with private bath; televisions but no telephones. Rates: moderate. Cards: MC, V, AE. Pets not permitted. Open all year.

Getting There: From the ferry dock follow the signs to Crescent Beach and the inn.

A Heady Spot

RAM'S HEAD INN
Shelter Island

In 1947 this grand and solid Center Hall Colonial with its fine view of harbor and bay was the site of the First Shelter Island Conference on the Foundations of Quantum Mechanics. Oppenheimer, Pauling, and a couple of dozen other scientists changed the basic structure of conceptualizing matter and created a new cosmology.

The second Shelter Island conference was held in June 1983, but the results were apparently not quite so dramatic. In any event, the Ram's Head Inn—with a namesake ram's head over the entrance—was a marvelous setting for both conferences. The terraced dining room and patio overlooking the sloping greenery leading past the inn tennis court and on to the harbor is a fine place for relaxing after a hard day's discussion. Or after a day of boating, fishing, swimming, and sunning—the summer specialties of Shelter Island.

The inn has a pair of thirteen-foot sloops for the use of guests and can arrange for bicycle rentals in town. They also have five moorings on their four acres of grounds, and there's a separate dinghy dock available for tying up when coming from boat to shore.

The rooms are furnished in country Colonial fashion with a welcome freshness about them. Among favorite rooms are Numbers 1 and 2, with more windows than the other rooms; Number 9 has some fine nautical prints.

The food is excellent and the wine list surprisingly good. The rooms have no such diversionary distractions as telephones, televisions, clocks, radios; so as the innkeeper here advises, "prepare yourself for a very relaxing experience letting the beauty of Shelter Island and the sunsets entertain you. Come, sit back and relax, we'll take good care of you."

RAM'S HEAD INN, Ram Island, Shelter Island, New York 11965. Telephone: (516) 749-0811. Accommodations: 9 rooms and four suites, most

with private bath; no televisions or telephones. Rates: inexpensive to moderate; includes Continental breakfast. Cards: MC, V. Inquire about pets. Open from first week in May to mid-October.

Getting There: From the Greenport ferry, the North Ferry, follow route 114A South, past the Mobil gas station to a left turn on Winthrop Road; on Cobbets Lane go to the end and turn left, then take the first right over the causeway to the inn.

Countrified Quiet
PECONIC LODGE
Shelter Island Heights

Families searching for reasonably priced holidays built around all kinds of water sports, along with tennis, badminton, and cycling, should consider the Peconic Lodge, located a few hundred meters from the Greenport ferry on Crescent Beach.

The Lodge will make arrangements to pick up guests at the ferry dock and will also provide mooring facilities for those who come by boat. Its own fleet of sail- and rowboats is available at their own beach—eight hundred feet of it—and there are beach chairs and umbrellas for waterfront sunning and sitting.

Within a hundred feet of that sandy beach there are single- and double-bedroom cabin accommodations with a separate lodge for families with small children. The modern housekeeping cottages have space for up to four guests, and there are equally modern rooms in the main lodge building.

Overlooking beach and bay is a splendid porch, a perfect place for an early evening gathering to swap stories about the day's activities, and get ready, with drinks in hand, to tackle the dining room with its solid offerings of food.

The tree-shaded cottages and bungalows, cooled by breezes from both Gardiners and Peconic bays, are appropriately informal for those who want total escape from the rigors of city life.

PECONIC LODGE, Shore Road, Shelter Island Heights, New York 11965. Telephone: (516) 749-0170. Accommodations: 39 rooms in the lodge, 22 cottages with kitchens, each with private bath; no televisions or telephones, but television in main lodge common room. Rates: inexpensive to moderate; European and modified American plan (breakfast and dinner) available. No cards. Pets not permitted. Open May 1 to mid-October.

24

Getting There: Follow Shore Road from the Greenport ferry dock to Crescent Beach and the inn.

Well Manored

TOWNSEND MANOR INN
Greenport

The Townsend Manor Inn opened in 1926, but the origins of the three buildings go back almost a century before that. In 1835 a successful whaling captain, George Cogswell, built, directly on the shores of Stirling Basin, a grand mansion with a four-pillared Greek Revival facade and spacious rooms. Today it's the main building of the Townsend complex, a three-acre spread of lawn and towering trees with a swimming pool and a marina, a cocktail lounge and dining rooms in a total of six buildings including a poolside snack bar, a waterfront cottage, and a water-view apartment all enclosed with hedges, neatly kept gardens, and white picket fences.

A favorite accommodation here is the Gingerbread House, with its high ceilings, round-the-corner windows, and Victorian trim. It's one of the architectural gems of the town and dates from 1843, when it was built as a home for the founder of the local bank of Greenport, Grosvenor Adams. The five rooms in the Captain's House are Colonial in design and furnishings. Most of the other rooms rambling across the grounds are more modern. The apartment units are ideal for vacationing families, including those who come by boat and those who want to take advantage of the reduced fees at a nearby golf course, play tennis, go sailing or fishing or just loaf around the pool.

Some of the rooms have kitchens and kitchenettes; others have refrigerators, and the dining room is open for three meals a day. The fare is solid: soup and sandwiches for lunch, and for dinner Yankee pot roast, sauerbraten, shell steaks and fried oysters, broiled or deep-fried scallops from Peconic Bay just a few hundred meters away.

At the town's main docks there's ferry boat service to Shelter Island, along with a variety of charter and sightseeing boats.

A few minutes east of Greenport on State Road 25, en route to a ferry terminal that serves New London connections, there's a wonderful timestood-still settlement known as Orient Point. Turn off the road at Village Lane, by the small obelisk erected in 1870 to honor Civil War dead, and drive about a half mile into history, into the era when Indians roamed the marshes and fields and Colonel George Washington and his Colonials marched through.

Townsend Manor Inn

Homes and offices are beautifully preserved, and there's a vintage country store next door to a red frame postage stamp of a post office. Oysterponds quilts are displayed in a neighboring home, and another store down the street, the Old Orchard Farm Store, now serves as a Girl Scout mini-museum. Across the Lane is the Methodist Church built in 1835, and there's a small park, Poquatuck, where the Indians camped.

George Washington really did sleep in the Webb House. It was built in 1740 but moved to the site in 1955 from Greenport and now serves as a fine local historical museum. Near the waters that earned Oysterponds its name is Shinbone Alley, an antique store of quality.

TOWNSEND MANOR INN, 714 Main Street, Greenport, New York 11944. Telephone: (516) 477-2000. Accommodations: 23 rooms and suites, each with private bath and television, some with kitchens or kitchenettes or refrigerators; telephones in all rooms. Rates: moderate. Cards: AE, MC, V. Pets not permitted. Full meal and bar service. Open all year (restaurant open April through November).

Getting There: On State Road 25, which is Front Street when it reaches Greenport, turn left (north) on Main Street and go four blocks to the inn on the right side of Main Street—a continuation of State Road 25.

Good Things Come in Threes

THREE VILLAGE INN
Stony Brook

The three villages are Stony Brook, Setauket, and Old Field, and reading from left to right that means harbor settings in tree-lined streets filled with nineteenth-century homes, a fine old gristmill, Federal-style shops. Setauket has one of Long Island's most comprehensive historic districts, with a 1729 Episcopal Church and a fine array of eighteenth-century homes, including the Thompson House from around 1700. This large frame structure is filled with early Long Island furniture and has a Colonial herb garden out back (open to the public May–October). Old Field is an estate area, with Long Island Sound on one side and Conscience Bay on the other.

Stony Brook also has the largest private museum on Long Island, a complex established in 1935 and consisting of the home of Long Island artist William Sidney Mount, a carriage museum with more than a hundred horse-drawn vehicles, an eighteenth-century barn, an art gallery, and fifteen miniature rooms depicting interior styles from the 1600s to the 1930s.

Stony Brook also has a fine row of carefully restored shops forming a crescent around the Village Green, directly across the street from the historic Three Village Inn. The core of the inn is the homestead Richard Hallock built in 1751; around it fans the white frame building with its distinctive green trim and its front patio for sitting and watching the action across the way on the green and over at the marina.

There are several rooms for guests in the main building, rooms which capture the spirit of the inn and its past. Number 1 has heavy beam rafters, fine old wrought-iron hardware, floral wallpaper, and a pair of comfortable overstuffed chairs. Out back, in little cottages under the tall trees, are more spacious, modern accommodations. They too are furnished with period pieces and carefully selected reproductions.

The inn's kitchen has earned a reputation in these three villages—and far beyond—for its imaginative approach to menus that just won't quit: would you believe 34 appetizers, 36 entrées, and 22 desserts—just for lunch?

Long-gowned smiling young women greet the guests noon and night (and at breakfast for inn guests only), serving them in the Colonial Sandbar Tap Room with its long wooden bar, its bull's-eye glass windows and brick fireplaces, crowned by heavy beams overhead; or in the more formal Colonial Dining Room.

As a small selection of what's featured in this splendid tribute to good taste, the back room serves hot and cold poached mussels; veal pâté remoulade; scallop seviche; fresh salmon, cod, flounder, bluefish, lobster, and soft-shell crabs; curried pork and sausage with wild rice en casserole; sweetbreads in a Madeira-mushroom sauce, baked colossal shrimp stuffed with crabmeat; braised beef with baby white onions on fried eggplant; and all kinds of seasonal fruits and berries, presented with cream or baked expertly into pies, cakes, and crisps.

THREE VILLAGE INN, 150 Main Street, Stony Brook, New York 11790. Telephone: (516) 751-0555. Accommodations: 33 rooms, each with private bath, television, and telephone. Rates: moderate. Cards: AE, CB, DC, MC, V. Pets not permitted. Open all year.

Getting There: The inn is in the center of town across from the village green.

NEW YORK CITY

A Country Inn in the City

ALGONQUIN

New York City

The flyer for this landmark hotel in the heart of midtown Manhattan declares that it's "the New York Hotel with all the endearing qualities of a Fine Inn."

Despite the size—two hundred rooms and suites—there is no argument with such a claim. The Algonquin, famed for its Round Table of a half century ago, is indeed a fine inn, or maybe a club where the literati still meet, and stars and would-be stars (and maybe a few has-beens and a good many never-wases) of stage, screen, and radio find companionship and comfort.

Alexander Woolcott, George S. Kaufman, Dorothy Parker, and Robert Benchley are long gone from the scene, but the Round Table spirit survives; in fact, it thrives in the one-of-a-kind lobby and the intimate little Blue Bar with its polished mahogany paneling and etched glass. And it thrives in the formal Rose Room where the meals are reliable and the service solicitous.

The guest rooms are comfortably appointed with brass beds, period pieces, and reproductions suitable to the atmosphere of a hostelry that has passed the 75-year mark.

Sipping tea on a late afternoon, having a drink in a corner of the lobby (just ring the brass bell to summon a waiter), or working through the Sunday "bruncheon" or the traditional late-night, post-theater supper buffet, one has the distinct feeling that this hotel is something special that does have "the endearing qualities of a Fine Inn."

ALGONQUIN, 59 West Forty-fourth Street, New York, New York 10036. Telephone: (212) 840-6800. Accommodations: 200 rooms and suites, each with private bath, television, and telephone. Rates: moderate to expensive. Cards: AE, CB, DC, MC, V. Inquire about pets. Open all year.

Getting There: The hotel is between Fifth Avenue and Avenue of the Americas.

Museum-Mile Americana
AMERICAN STANHOPE
New York City

Overlooking Central Park, a few feet away from the Metropolitan Museum of Art and a short distance from the Guggenheim and the Cooper-Hewitt museums, is this American classic, an antique-filled joy to behold and to experience.

There are paintings and prints galore detailing the glories of the American past, the smallest of lobbies to guarantee the privacy of the guests, free limousine service to midtown Manhattan, handsomely appointed rooms with color-coordinated fabrics and wall coverings, important accent pieces, well-crafted reproductions, and an overall feeling of country inn comfort—and pampering.

Sit in a velvet Victorian rocker and contemplate a nineteenth-century landscape or relax in the arms of a cozy couch while reviewing a day of museum-going, or shopping. All around the Stanhope are the myriad fascinations of the city that has it all—uptown, downtown, East Side, West Side, two hundred years old and last-week new—many only blocks away. You'll welcome the walk if you've over-indulged in the Stanhope's dining rooms.

One of them, the Furnished Room, is named for a story by O. Henry, whose portrait graces one wall; another recaptures the past with a parade of paintings. That's the Saratoga, a personal favorite. But in summers there's no better spot to relax after a day at the Metropolitan or in the shops, resting a bit before taking on the theater, than the Terrace, a sidewalk cafe of considerable class.

No matter where one decides to dine here, disappointment will not be on the menu. Executive chef Jerome Collins, steeped in the *nouvelle* American cuisine approach of the California crowd as well as of Paul Prudhomme and other masters of the Cajun-Creole kitchen, arrived on the scene in July 1984.

Buffalo burgers, littleneck clams on a circle of seaweed, oysters from wherever they're best at the time, pan-fried chicken, freshly picked vegetables and fruits, all kinds of cobblers, and strawberry shortcake—those are some of the headliners, and you'll want to toast your good fortune in finding chef Collins's creations with a drink or two in the adjoining lounge named after the Indian chief Red Jacket.

AMERICAN STANHOPE, 995 Fifth Avenue (at Eighty-first Street), New York, New York 10028. Telephone: (212) 288-5800. Accommodations: 160 rooms, each with private bath, television, and telephone. Rates: very expensive. Cards: AE, CB, DC, MC, V. Open all year.

Getting There. The inn is across the street from the Metropolitan Museum of Art.

Sheer Class
NO. 1022
New York City

The same realtor, retailer, restaurateur, and all-round entrepreneur who transformed the one-hundred-room Sonoma Mission Inn and Spa into the class act of the California wine country, the same Edward J. Safdie who revitalized the seventy-five-room Norwich Inn in the Connecticut town of the same name, has applied the same Midas touch to this enclave of exclusivity on the corner of Lexington Avenue and East 73rd Street.

Behind the buff-white facade of No. 1022 Lexington there are three suites and a studio designed for guests who want maximum privacy for an extended period of time—and are willing to pay for it. Daily rentals are in the $200–$400 range, monthly from $4,000 to $7,000, or about the same rate as New York's Plaza.

But there's far more privacy at No. 1022 than in the always-bustling Plaza, along with TV security front door monitors, microwave ovens in self-contained kitchens, private telephone lines, Jacuzzis, and daily chauffeur, maid, and food service. The interiors were designed by London-born, New York-based Georgina Fairholme, who created the best-dressed rooms in this book, complete with terraces, skylights, fireplaces.

Handpainted silk pillows luxuriate on sofas and chairs in pretty pastels of azure blue, apple green, melon, and lemon. Canopy beds have Shaker pencil posts, slipper chairs are upholstered in bright English chintz, and there are antiques and accent pieces such as porcelain figurines by English artist Lady Anne Gordon. Mirrored panels hide the closets, and the woodwork in parts is marbleized, but nowhere is there any sense of over-decorating. Georgina Fairholme did not crowd, nor did she create a setting of remote formality where a guest does not feel at home.

On the ground floor of the inn is Jacks, a black and white, polished-brass restaurant with offerings that epitomize the New American cuisine—many of which are low-calorie dishes from Safdie's new spas in Arlington, Texas, and Monte Carlo, Monaco: garden greens with goat cheese, grilled rabbit sausage on fennel coulis, Cajun grilled salmon, roast leg of veal with ginger and wild mushrooms, roasted partridge with pear sauce and some not-so-new nor diet-conscious desserts such as a banana split.

No. 1022, 1022 Lexington Avenue, New York, New York 10021. Telephone: (212) 697-1536. Accommodations: three suites and one studio, each with private bath, television, telephone. Rates: very expensive; includes stocked kitchen for do-it-yourself breakfasts and snacks. Cards: AE, CB, DC, MC, V. Inquire about children; no pets. Open all year.

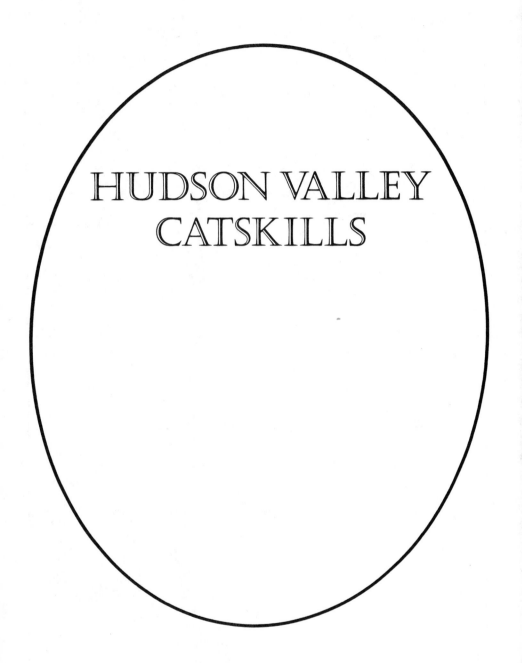

HUDSON VALLEY
CATSKILLS

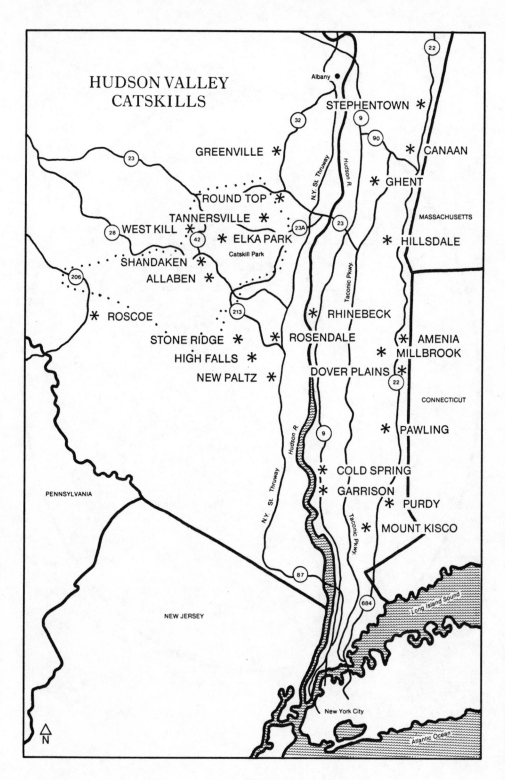

HUDSON VALLEY
CATSKILLS

Albany

STEPHENTOWN ✱

CANAAN ✱

GREENVILLE ✱

GHENT ✱

ROUND TOP ✱

TANNERSVILLE ✱

WEST KILL ✱

ELKA PARK ✱

HILLSDALE ✱

Catskill Park

SHANDAKEN ✱

ALLABEN ✱

MASSACHUSETTS

RHINEBECK ✱

✱ ROSCOE

STONE RIDGE ✱

ROSENDALE ✱

AMENIA ✱

MILLBROOK ✱

HIGH FALLS ✱

NEW PALTZ ✱

DOVER PLAINS ✱

CONNECTICUT

PAWLING ✱

COLD SPRING ✱

GARRISON ✱

PURDY ✱

MOUNT KISCO ✱

PENNSYLVANIA

NEW JERSEY

Long Island Sound

New York City

Atlantic Ocean

N. Y. St. Thruway

Hudson R.

Taconic Pkwy.

N. Y. St. Thruway

Hudson R.

Taconic Pkwy.

23

32

9

90

23

23A

42

28

206

213

22

22

9

87

684

N

HUDSON VALLEY

Closest to the City
THE KITTLE HOUSE
Mount Kisco

A Westchester landmark with more plusses than most inns can boast: it's close to two centuries old; it sports a bar no less a personage than Fanny Brice brought into the country; it has a marvelous stone fireplace in the lounge (and live entertainment on the weekends); it's surrounded by seven acres of woods and gardens; it's the closest country inn to New York City. And, most important of all if you're interested in food, it's now owned and operated by the Crabtrees.

The Crabtree clan—Dick, John, Clare, Mimi—is very much in evidence and together they have worked a miracle of restoration, sprucing up lounge and dining room, refurbishing the upstairs rooms, putting new life into a building whose architectural style might best be described as Old Barn.

They've also installed a new menu, with a Sunday brunch, and croissant and Monte Cristo sandwiches for lunch. Other dishes include omelets made with Boursin cheese, smoked salmon, and sautéed onion, and a marvelous curried chicken salad showered with almonds and coconut, garnished with kiwi, papaya, and avocado.

Dinners at Crabtree's Kittle House start with escargots Paul Bocuse (tomato, basil, cream sauce), smoked salmon roll, cheese fritters, or asparagus puffs, and are followed by tournedos garnished with prosciutto and chives sautéed in Madeira wine, plume de veau, duckling on a bed of stuffing, or calves' liver sautéed with ginger.

Summer activities in the Mount Kisco area include the five-week lively arts festival known as Summerfare, which is held at Purchase and hosted by

Kittle House

the State University of New York. At nearby Katonah there's an annual Caramoor Music Festival from the end of June to the end of August (Caramoor also houses an excellent art gallery and museum) and in Port Chester in the Ward Castle there's a Museum of Cartoon Art; Sunnyside was the home of Washington Irving and is located in Tarrytown not far distant.

THE KITTLE HOUSE, Route 117, Mt. Kisco, New York 10549. Telephone: (914) 666-8044. Accommodations: 17 rooms, each with private bath, television, and telephone; one room with refrigerator; some rooms with large walk-in closets. Rates: moderate; includes Continental breakfast. Full meal and bar service. Cards: AC, CB, DC, MC, V. Pets permitted, but inquire first. Open all year.

Getting There: From the Mt. Kisco exit of the Sawmill Parkway, take Readers Digest Road to Route 117. Turn left on 117 and follow just a half mile to the inn on the right hand side of the road.

Fabulous Food

BOX TREE
Purdy's

A weekend at this historic old home is, arguably, the greatest gastronomic experience in this book. Arrive in time for dinner and you will find Pernod-soaked snails, shrimp and tomatoes in a dill remoulade, fish sausage or calves' brains showered with capers, followed by entrées of beef with cognac or green peppercorns, veal scallops with morels in cream, sweetbreads in a truffle sauce, or a duckling in a honey-lime sauce.

The meal will be consumed in a setting that vibrates with the past. Ten years ago, when the original wood was exposed, that past—all the way back to 1775—was laid bare: the heavy hand-hewn beams, the wide-plank floors, the carved railings.

A steep stairway leads to the second-floor suite, an antique-filled accommodation with a bed that once belonged to French King Francis I, with a Canadian lynx fur throw, and a Queen Anne dining room where a multicourse breakfast is presented—a brace of roast quail with croissants and brioches is the usual, along with fruits and some kind of egg creation.

The dining room downstairs was once the kitchen, and it has an oversized hearth dominating one wall; the former library is now the bar, and out back the Box Tree's Austrian chef, Rudi Granser, works his wonders.

It's all a mission to the provinces by restaurateur Augustin V. Paege, who has a notable restaurant in Manhattan at 250 East Forty-ninth Street, also known as the Box Tree.

In the country, the desserts are slightly more traditional, with the Viennese Granser producing Linzertorte along with a cake of chocolate mousse and a vacherin Box Tree built around a hazelnut-meringue torte laden with strawberries and heavy cream.

There's an adequate selection of cheeses, along with a fine array of vintage ports and top-label brandies and cognacs. The wine list is also carefully chosen.

THE BOX TREE, P. O. Box 77, Purdy's, New York 10578. Telephone: (914) 277-3677. Accommodations: one room and one suite, each with private bath; no televisions or telephones. Rates: very expensive; includes full breakfast. No cards. Children not permitted; no pets. Open all year.

Getting There: At the Purdy's exit of Interstate 684, follow State Road 22/116 a few hundred meters to where the white two-story inn is clearly marked with a sign.

George Should Have Slept Here

BIRD & BOTTLE INN
Garrison

An hour's drive from the George Washington Bridge is this time capsule from pre-Revolutionary America, the era of stagecoaches and rugged roads, redcoats and rebels. In 1761 the inn was opened as Warren's Tavern; a few years later it was in the center of the encampment of the Colonials protecting the Hudson Highlands. In the next century it was converted into a farmhouse and a hundred years later into a handsomely furnished inn.

Ever since the Bird & Bottle opened in 1940, it's been noted for its fine kitchen. At noontime that means homemade breads layered thickly with Cheddar, or top sirloin and Bermuda onion rings, or chicken and tarragon. At night, after a cup of the excellent house special of black bean soup, there's duckling Bigarade; roast pheasant in a sauce Perigueux freckled with truffles; tournedos Rossini; or a delectable chicken breast sautéed and then deglazed with sherry, mingled with prosciutto, thyme and mushrooms, finished with a rich brown sauce and a splash of thick cream. On Sundays there's a bountiful brunch featuring such specials as country French toast, London broil, Chicken Divan, country pâté bathed in Cumberland sauce, and fresh fruit soaked in Kirshwasser.

A few years ago, a cozy little cottage and the second-floor rooms were beautifully restored, filled with period pieces, four-posters or canopied beds, and working fireplaces.

The nearby Boscobel Restoration with its magnificent gardens and its perfect state of restoration and furnishings is the finest example of Federal interior design and domestic architecture in the state.

There are other restored mansions and estates in Sleepy Hollow Country. That name was given to the Hudson Valley by the genius who wrote about the legends and the lore of this land, Washington Irving. His home at Sunnyside, still "as full of angles and corners as an old cocked hat," has been carefully restored, as have two outstanding examples of Dutch Colonial wealth, power, and taste: Philipsburg Manor in North Tarrytown, with a working gristmill and a marvelous manor-house kitchen, and Van Cortlandt Manor at Croton-on-Hudson, considered to be one of the most authentic restorations of early Colonial life. There are well-kept eighteenth-century gardens and a ferry house built in 1688.

Lyndhurst in Tarrytown, a property of the National Trust for Historic Preservation, reflects a far different era, that of the Gothic castle craze. Among the owners was that quintessential expression of the Gilded Age, Jay Gould.

BIRD & BOTTLE INN, Route 9, Garrison, New York 10524. Telephone: (914) 424-3000. Accommodations: four rooms, each with private bath; no televisions or telephones. Rates: moderate. Cards: AE, MC, V. Pets not permitted. Open all year (but November through April closed Monday and Tuesday).

Getting There: From the Peekskill exit of the Taconic Parkway, follow State Road 202 three miles to Bear Mountain Parkway to State Road 9, following that road eight miles to the inn.

Good as Gold
GOLDEN EAGLE INN
Garrison's Landing

The only time you might not want to come to this three-story brick historic hostelry is the third weekend in August, when some ten thousand other travelers descend on the crossroads of a town for the annual arts and crafts show.

Other times of the year it's considerably more tranquil, and the inn, which has been opening its doors to guests since the 1840s, is a perfect little retreat. Guests can spend their time breakfasting or brunching on the ver-

Golden Eagle Inn

andah or inside in the invitingly cozy cafe, gathering for drinks (BYOB) at the end of the day, watching the sun set over the distant highlands, watching the river roll lazily along, or discussing art, design, sailing, skiing, shooting, and just about everything else with innkeeper George Templeton, an enthusiast of the first rank and an artist of considerable talent.

His water colors of sleek sloops and lushly landscaped Hilton Head golf courses are much in evidence and are, along with other artworks, for sale. He also works a bit in bronze and wood—as in the cross-country skis propped up in a corner.

With wife Stephanie, George over the past dozen years has transformed his pride and joy, which is directly across the Hudson from West Point, into an inn of honest appeal. Each of the rooms is individually decorated, and blends in beautifully with the park-like surroundings. And if it all looks rather familiar to you as you drive up the road a few meters from the railroad station, then you're probably a fan of the movie *Hello Dolly*. It was filmed at the Golden Eagle. Look for the grandly etched "Vandergelder" on the front glass.

Food here is not quite as elaborate as that served in the movie's banquet, but George has fun with the menu, serving Riverboat sandwiches, midnight chocolate cake, "Treats and Trifles" for lunch, and a "Breadley Medley" of homemade baked goods. A final plus—George will also guide you to the attractions of the area, point out where the boat and canoe are kept, and where the best cross-country trails and the best antique stores are.

GOLDEN EAGLE INN, Garrison's Landing, New York 10524. Telephone: (914) 424-3067. Accommodations: five rooms, three with private bath, two with shared bath; no televisions or telephones. Rates: moderate; includes Continental breakfast. Cards: AE, MC, V; cash preferred. Children not permitted; no pets. Open April 1 to January 1.

Getting There: The inn is exactly 50 miles by train from New York City—the local station is across from the inn. By car it is six-tenths of a mile west of the junction of State Roads 9D and 403.

A Waterfront Winner
HUDSON HOUSE
Cold Spring

Innkeeper Mary Pat Bevis must have poured lots of love into this sensationally revitalized inn, the second oldest in continuous operation in the state. It's a case study in restoration, an important addition to the history-conscious landscape of Cold Spring, which was given that name, according to the story, by George Washington when he stopped to water his horse. That took place a few feet away from the inn, on the banks of the Hudson River, near where the little bandstand of a gazebo now stands as a fitting ornament to the charm of Cold Spring.

The Half Moon Bar in the inn is named after the ship of those who went ashore to explore during Henry Hudson's time. Another echo of the past is in the quilting patterns used in the rooms with cheerful abandon, and even for the holders of the room keys. It's a nice extra touch. So is the old-fashioned ice cream parlor and the dining room, lined with windows to look out on the mighty Hudson.

History has been kept in the Hudson House, but modern amenities were not overlooked—all the bathrooms are new, and the balconies of rooms facing the river have been restored and reinforced, so that a guest in one of those rooms with a paddle fan overhead and period reproductions all about can have a fine view of West Point, and woods and mountains that must have looked the same to Washington and Hudson.

HUDSON HOUSE, 2 Main Street, Cold Spring, New York 10516. Telephone: (914) 265-9355. Accommodations: 14 rooms, each with private bath; no televisions or telephones; suite; twin, double, and queen size beds. Rates: moderate; includes Continental breakfast. Full bar and meal service. Cards: MC, V. Open February through December.

Getting There: The inn is on the town's main street a few hundred feet from the Hudson.

Simply Suite

ONE MARKET STREET
Cold Spring

On the corner of Main and Market streets, across from the far larger Hudson House, is this very personal single suite rented out by the proprietors of the dream of a shop on the ground floor, Philip and Esther Baumgarten.

The solid brick building with the distinctive bay window dates from the 1830s and is known as the Hudson Peddler. In this little hideaway a block from the Hudson River the Baumgartens sell all kinds of gifts and collectibles, along with some antiques and souvenirs of the Cold Spring area.

Behind and upstairs is a very spacious, comfortably furnished suite with a fully stocked kitchen. The carefully kept garden adds to the enjoyment of staying in this centrally located building that honors the past so proudly.

ONE MARKET STREET, 1 Market Street, Cold Spring, New York 10516. Telephone: (914) 265-3912. Accommodations: one suite with private bath and fully stocked kitchen; no television or telephone. Rates: moderate. Cards: MC, V. Inquire about pets. Open all year.

Getting There: The inn is on the main street one block from the Hudson River.

A Spotless Budget-Pleaser

GUESTS
Pawling

No inn book would be complete without a few simple establishments for those who want to remain on the budget trail. Guests, immaculately maintained by owner Ines Venezia, is precisely that kind of place, a two-story home on the highway southeast of Poughkeepsie, with a large porch for sitting and relaxing and a quiet, small town ambiance.

For a similarly inexpensive outing, there's Lake Walton Park at Hopewell Junction some twenty miles west of Pawling. It has a twenty-acre picnic grove with a sandy beach and a bathhouse, boat rentals, recreation areas, and camping facilities ringing a fifty-acre spring-fed lake.

GUESTS, Route 22, Pawling, New York 12564. Telephone: (914) 878-6286. Accommodations: five rooms with shared baths; no televisions or telephones; one room with kitchenette. Rates: inexpensive. No cards. Pets not permitted. Open all year.

Getting There: The inn is on State Road 22 between Haviland and Hurds Corners, a couple of miles from the Connecticut border.

From Cattle to Curries

OLD DROVERS INN
Dover Plains

Our thumb-worn Webster explains that a drover is one who drives cattle to market, and though the drovers of New England, guiding their herds along the Post Road (State Road 22) to the important market in New York City, are long gone, their memory lives on in this grand and ultra-comfortable inn.

Opened in 1750 as the Clear Water Tavern by the Preston brothers, John and Ebenezer, the inn was purchased during the Depression by Olin Chester Potter—he changed the name to Old Drovers and started serving food that soon brought in the crowds and impressed the critics.

Old Drovers Cheddar cheese soup is the proper beginning to a feast in the beamed taproom with its distinctive hurricane glass globes softly filtering the flickering candlelight. Follow this with the partridge or the pheasant, all raised on neighboring farms and prepared in the kitchen with great skill and conscience. Or you might prefer one of their special curries.

The wine cellar is well stocked, and guests today drink a far higher quality of rum and ale than those early drovers. And they also sleep in considerably more luxurious surroundings: thick comforters and quilts, matching bath linens, cheerful fires, antiques and handsome accent pieces.

Mornings at this inn start with breakfast served on mahogany tables in a second-floor haven called the Federal Room. The wall murals look as though they've been there since John Adams's time; they depict the surrounding countryside, the inn, and the Hyde Park mansion of the Roosevelts.

OLD DROVERS INN, Old Drovers Inn Road, Dover Plains, New York 12522. Telephone: (914) 832-9311. Accommodations: three rooms, each with private bath; no televisions or telephones. Rates: expensive. Cards: AE. Children not encouraged; no pets. Open Thursday through Monday all year except for three weeks in December.

Getting There: The inn is a half mile off State Road 22, three miles south of the little town of Dover Plains and four miles north of Wingdale.

Old Drovers Inn

A Revitalized Retreat

COTTONWOOD INN
Millbrook

In January 1983 new owners Sandra and Bob DiLuca took over this quiet little highway hugger southwest of the—"sweet" might be the operative word to describe it—village with its mid-town tribute to the veterans of World War I laid out by the local garden club. The DiLucas worked a complete renovation, and the main building now sparkles with white paint, as perhaps it did when it was first built in 1790.

With non-greedy rates, the Cottonwood represents a reasonably priced base camp, though not as inexpensive as the Twin Maples, for exploring the countryside (see the Twin Maples commentary).

COTTONWOOD INN, Route 44, Millbrook, New York 12545. Telephone: (914) 677-3919. Accommodations: 14 rooms, each with private bath; televisions; no telephones. Rates: inexpensive. Cards: AE, MC, V. Pets not permitted. Open all year.

Getting There: The inn is 2.3 miles from the intersection of U.S. 44 with State Roads 82/343, on the road from Millbrook to Washington Hollow.

A Baronial Decorator's Dream
TROUTBECK
Amenia

The land was first settled about the time George Washington was leaving the Presidency, and in the years before the Civil War it was given its present name, christened by noted naturalist Myron Benton, a friend of John Burroughs, Emerson, and Thoreau. It was Burroughs who once wrote about such natural, wooded retreats: "I come here to find myself; it is so easy to get lost in the world."

At the end of World War I, Joel Spingarn, a noted horticulturist and literary critic, built a Tudor manor on the property, massing mountains of cut stone under gabled roofs of slate, with luxurious landscaping in a setting of woods, magnificent sky-high sycamores planted by Benton, a dozen springs, the meandering Webatuck River, and a brook.

"Troutbeck still offers a link between a family and a landscape, between a patch of historic soil and the generations that are still to come," wrote neighbor Lewis Mumford in the 1920s. That's the time when Troutbeck was the rallying point for the likes of Charles Lindbergh and liberals and literati Langston Hughes, Booker T. Washington, and W.E.B. DuBois. DuBois founded the NAACP at Spingarn's estate.

After World War II Troutbeck was abandoned and for three decades it slowly decayed. But then Robert Skibsted and James Flaherty, a pair of international marketing and copywriting pros, took over. That was in 1978, and since that time they have not only revitalized the manor and all its parts; they have restored the formal walled gardens, planting everything from primroses to petunias.

They have also installed a kitchen of great merit, one that turns out Saturday night roast beef–Yorkshire pudding meals without peer. Other specialties include fresh salmon poached with a dill-enhanced hollandaise, crisp duck, tournedos, lobster, escargots, stuffed flounder, and a variety of breads, muffins, and evil desserts made fresh daily.

There's an open bar policy—the bottles are found on a tea cart and there are no chits to sign; it's all included in the cost of the accommodation, along with 422 acres of parklike grounds, tennis courts, a covered, heated winter pool and a beautiful new summer pool, as well as all kinds of trails for hiking or skiing, and a decorator's dream of interior design.

Fireplaces blaze merrily, there's a wealth of wonderful fabric on chairs and couches, rich wooden wall paneling, leaded windows, and a dramatic use of floral arrangements. Guest rooms, twelve of them in the Tudor manor house, another eighteen in an adjoining eighteenth-century farmhouse

49

reached by a stone bridge and called the Century, have canopy or four-poster beds and four have fireplaces. Lewis Mumford described the place best: "Troutbeck itself gives a sense of being snug, protected, inviolate."

Inngoers can find that secure solitude only on the weekends, however. Troutbeck during the week is an executive retreat utilized by a constant parade of the movers and shakers of the Fortune 500. It easily ranks as one of the most exclusive such enclaves in the country. And on the weekends—with reservations absolutely mandatory—Troutbeck easily ranks as one of the finest inns in the world.

TROUTBECK, Leedsville Road, Amenia, New York 12501. Telephone: (914) 373-8581. Accommodations: 30 rooms, most with private bath; no televisions or telephones. Rates: very expensive; includes all meals, open bar. Cards: AE. Children only under 1 or over 14 permitted; no pets. Open for inn guests only on weekends (from Friday dinner through Sunday brunch) and with reservations only.

Getting There: At the sign memoralizing Myron Benton's connection with Troutbeck, turn off State Road 343 (which runs five miles from Amenia to Sharon, Connecticut) onto Leedsville Road and to the inn.

Oldest in America!
BEEKMAN ARMS
Rhinebeck

Longfellow's Wayside Inn in Massachusetts argues the point, but the proprietors here consider their historic hostelry the oldest inn in the country, one that has been hosting guests since 1766. Shortly before the Revolution, the old two-room inn was replaced by a larger structure, and around that stone fortresslike core, the Beekman Arms has grown gradually to its present size.

But the past is not forgotten. In the splendid taproom with its massive overhead beams and wide-plank floors, the walls speak of the great ones who have passed through, from Washington and Lafayette to the Roosevelts.

Rhinebeck is just north of Roosevelt country, a half dozen miles from Hyde Park where, in a grand old home overlooking the Hudson, Franklin D. Roosevelt was born. The home, a National Historic Site, houses a library of presidential mementos and documents. Close by is Val-Kill, an 180-acre escape where wife Eleanor used to recoup and recover after her vigorous endeavors.

Between the Beekman Arms and Hyde Park there's another National Historic Site, the Vanderbilt Mansion designed by the firm of McKim, Mead and White in an Italian Renaissance style. Operated by the National Park Service, the *palazzo* provides dramatic insight into the lifestyles of the super-rich in the days of the Gilded Age.

In recent years Hyde Park has become famous for more than the Roosevelts and the Vanderbilts, however. It's gained considerable fame for its food, due to the presence of the Culinary Institute of America. Make a pilgrimage to a CIA of a different *modus operandi*, eat in their dining room, and learn for yourself why there has been such a *nouvelle* American cuisine revolution in hotel and restaurant kitchens.

At the Beekman Arms you'll experience the old-style American cuisine—prime rib, a variety of veal dishes, duck, and seafood. Breakfast, lunch, and dinner are served daily, and there's a Sunday brunch.

And if you're planning to eat or overnight at the Beekman Arms during the last weekend in June, reserve well in advance. That's the time of the annual Arts and Crafts Fair at the Dutchess County Fairgrounds in town, when well over three hundred craftsmen and artists descend on Rhinebeck, along with clowns and musicians and thousands of tourists.

BEEKMAN ARMS, Route 9, Rhinebeck, New York 12572. Telephone: (914) 876-7077. Accommodations: 37 rooms, 20 with private bath; some televisions; telephones. Rates: moderate. Cards: AE, DC, MC, V. Pets not permitted. Open all year.

Getting There: The inn is in the center of town on State Road 9.

Country Haute Cuisine
L'HOSTELLERIE BRESSANE
Hillsdale

It's the classic combination: a chef-husband behind the burners, his wife out front manning the register, overseeing the serving staff. In this case it's Jean Morel (he's the chef-proprietaire) and Madeleine Morel (she's the directrice-proprietaire). In 1971 they moved to this quiet crossroads, transforming a solidly built brick two-story with Palladian windows and no fewer than nine fireplaces into an enclave of Gallic excellence.

The inn building celebrated its bicentennial in 1983. This is where chef Morel holds his cooking classes, four-day intensive courses that can include all meals and accommodations or simply the midday meal. Classes run from 10:00 to 2:30 and break for lunch until 4:00, when there's an hour-long question-answer session. On Fridays students check into the kitchen at 5:30 pm and stay until the last guest is served dinner.

And those dinners run the gamut of Gallic glories, as we learned when working through a superb soufflé of chicken livers with just the right, light, touch of garlic. That was followed by one of the better interpretations of the standard French onion soup. Chef Morel uses egg yolks, then spikes the brew with cognac and Madeira. His pea soup also smashes the blah barriers: he uses a sprinkle of sorrel, consommé, and *crème frâiche*. His mushroom soup, an occasional nightly special, is marvelous, more of a bisque than a broth.

Also notable are his braised sweetbreads mingled with chestnuts in a fine port wine sauce, and the breast and thigh of duck, slightly rare in the manner of *nouvelle cuisine*. Accompanying vegetables—broccoli, carrots, spears of white turnips—are lightly steamed and crunchy, and the dessert table is a sensation. Filled with flowers and with the *au courant* Villeroy-Boch china, the offerings are impossible to resist. The cakes are super-rich, the lemon sherbet is served in lemon halves, and the floating islands are suspended in Grand Marnier.

The wine list is superb, with most of the great wines of Morel's native France represented, along with just three outsiders, among them Robert Mondavi, of course, and his high-flying 1974 Cabernet. There are sixteen Cognac selections and a half dozen Armagnacs.

What could be better than a swirl of the aromatic grape in a room with exposed-brick walls, a pewter chandelier, a grand tile-framed fireplace, flowers and candlelight, and the feeling of being hidden away in the kind of Colonial tavern that Lafayette's chef might have operated.

The upstairs rooms, simply furnished, do not destroy the mood: the roughly finished walls, the oversize armoires, the scattering of antiques and artifacts collected over the years by the Morels all combine to create the atmosphere of a French country inn.

L'HOSTELLERIE BRESSANE, corner of Routes 22 and 23 (P.O. Box 387), Hillsdale, New York 12529. Telephone: (518) 325-3412. Accommodations: six rooms; two with private bath, four sharing baths; no televisions or telephones. Rates: moderate to expensive; includes Continental breakfast. No cards. Full bar and meal service. Pets not permitted. Open all year except for February and March or April.

Getting There: The inn, with its sign out front, is at the intersection of State Roads 22 and 23 in Hillsdale.

Bavarian in the Berkshires
SWISS HUTTE
Hillsdale

In the summer and fall it's a riot of color, a beautiful blooming bit of the Berkshires with its own putting green and several golf courses near at hand, a swimming pool and beaches on a brook-fed pond, tennis courts and all kinds of hiking trails and opportunities for sitting and sunning. In the wintertime it's a white wonderland overlooking the Catamount ski area. Cross-country trails web the area.

Innkeepers Linda and Tom Breen might have moved the entire facility over from some ski center in Germany or Switzerland. They have created an atmosphere that is definitely Old World lodge/resort on a restrained scale. Their gardens are idyllic, their housekeeping impeccable, and their French kitchen, which produces three meals daily for the general public as well as for inn guests, is reliable, consistent, and award-winning—and with good reason.

The dining areas are cheerful enclaves at any time of the day, and the guest rooms are well appointed in modern motel style. Six of the rooms have individual patios, and six on the second level have private balconies looking out on the beauties of the surrounding Berkshire countryside.

Close by is Tanglewood, with its music festival each summer, and there are many antique shops in the immediate area.

SWISS HUTTE, Route 23, Hillsdale, New York 12529. Telephone: (518) 325-3333. Accommodations: 21 rooms, each with private bath and television; no telephones, one suite with fireplace; others with two bedrooms and one bath. Rates: moderate; modified American plan (breakfast and dinner). Cards: MC, V. Pets permitted. Open all year except month of April and November 15 to December 15.

Getting There: From the Hillsdale Exit of the Taconic State Parkway take State Road 23 ten miles east directly to the inn, looking carefully for the sign on the road leading down a slope to the main building.

Shaker Simplicity
THE INN AT THE SHAKER MILL FARM
Canaan

For those escapists who want to avoid the high-calorie, *haute cuisine* approach to life in a country inn, this three-story fieldstone retreat cum gristmill is the perfect answer.

Built by the Shakers in 1824 and restored with Shaker-inspired simplicity by noted furniture-maker Ingram Paperny a century and a half later, the inn in the foothills of the Berkshires is a fine place to leave behind the crowded life of the city.

Hang your clothes on a Shaker peg, sleep contentedly on a Shaker bed, walk along the stream and study the waterfall which once powered the grinding stones for the industrious, inventive Shakers who settled in this area, and across the border (five miles away) in Massachusetts. Their Hancock Village at the junction of Routes 20 and 41 west of Pittsfield, which they established in 1790, is an excellent place to study the simple, celibate ways of the Shakers. All summer long there are craftspeople at work in the twenty buildings, including the massive round stone barn, built two years after the inn.

Paperny, who sincerely believes that his inn is an extension of himself, added a sauna and a large second-floor lounge with a circular fireplace, utilized for do-it-yourself steak grilling.

"Our food is good and plentiful—too plentiful, perhaps, but that is our way," Paperny explains, adding that dress is always casual and that "those

The Inn at Shaker Mill Farm

who cherish the gentle joys of leisure may well find us to their liking; those looking for programmed pleasures would be wise to look elsewhere."

He has a multitude of books and magazines, a good collection of records, and near at hand is what he calls the "packaged culture" of Tanglewood, along with horses for hire, hiking trails, Queechy Lake for swimming, Jiminy Peak and Brodie Mountain for skiing, their own frozen pond for ice skating, and all kinds of cross-country trails.

Most of the inn guests are weekenders, and there are special rates for a full American plan: two breakfasts, two lunches, two dinners with a BYOB policy and the active discouragement of smoking in the dining room.

THE INN AT THE SHAKER MILL FARM, Cherry Lane, Canaan, New York 12029. Telephone: (518) 794-9345. Accommodations: 15 rooms, 13 with private bath; no televisions or telephones. Rates: moderate; includes breakfast. Cards: MC, V. Open all year.

Getting There: Cherry Lane is closer to New Lebanon than Canaan, 1.5 miles south of New Lebanon on State Road 22.

Alpine Excellence

MILLHOF INN
Stephentown

"Welcome to the only Stephentown on earth" is the greeting one gets when entering this settlement so close to the Massachusetts border—only five hundred feet away—it could almost be in a New England inns book. They should be so lucky.

Stephentown is a fun place at any time of the year—whether you are booked into the Tanglewood Music Festival, or want to pass the leaf season in the Berkshires, or attend the Williamstown Theatre Festival, or zoom down the slopes at Jiminy Peak or Brodie Mountain when the world turns white.

The Hancock Shaker Village is just to the south across the border, and in New York, at Old Chatham southwest of Stephentown, there's another Shaker museum spread out in eight buildings, including exhibitions of the Shaker inventive genius, a museum store with a fine selection of books and pamphlets about every aspect of the sect, which is officially known as The United Society of Believers in Christ's Second Appearing—founded by Mother Ann Lee outside of Albany in the 1770s.

Mother Lee decreed that "There is no dust in heaven," and that same sense of order and cleanliness is what one finds in the Millhof, given that name because it was once a sawmill. It was transformed with liberal doses of TLC with a spicing of the old country—innkeepers Romana and Frank Tallet are obviously inspired with memories of their native countries of Yugoslavia and France.

The individually decorated rooms are filled with imports, books, and memorabilia, and there's a library on the ground floor, along with a fireplace where guests gather to read, to exchange travel stories, and to listen to good music. In a small new (1981) section added to the original building there's a splendid bridal suite with corner and bay windows overlooking the tidily kept garden and a small pool.

Breakfast and lunch are served on the Garden Deck and in a charming little room the Tallets have christened the Europa. Chef Romana does the cooking, and her Central European–Yugoslav background shows in her various specialties. Breakfast is served to non-overnight guests, but dinners are only for those staying at this excellent Alpine chalet, which provides complimentary afternoon tea to guests.

MILLHOF INN, Route 43, Stephentown, New York 12168; mailing address: P.O. Box 79, Hancock, Massachusetts 01237. Telephone: (518) 733-5606. Accommodations: ten rooms and a suite, each with private bath; no televisions or telephones. Rates: moderate; includes afternoon tea and Continental breakfast. Cards: AE, MC, V. Children under 12 not permitted; no pets. Open from last week in May through the end of March.

Getting There: From the junction of State Roads 43 East and 22 North, go 1.2 miles east on 43 directly to the inn.

CATSKILLS

THE CATSKILLS

The Catskills is a land of startling contrasts, a land of blaring discos and quiet mountain streams, of Borscht Circuit big names and binocular-wielding birdwatchers, a three-thousand-square-mile spread of forest and farmland dotted with such giants of the hospitality world as Grossinger's, a 650-room, eight-hundred-acre Tudor monster that's the oldest of the ten or so surviving resort-hotels. They all started out as boardinghouses, and in a decade there were forty or fifty of them. Typically, the same families, the fourth generation, are still in charge.

Then there's Aunt Lil, in charge of Brown's Hotel, with its 260 acres in the midst of spectacular scenery, and such showcase performers as Jerry Lewis, Steve and Eydie, Shecky Greene, and Rita Moreno.

Each indoor event has a hundred alternatives outdoors. You can ski the Big Cats—Hunter Mountain, Cortina Valley, Ski Windham, White Birches, North Lake, Hyer Meadows—and fish the newly cleaned-up Hudson, angling for bass, shad, herring, sturgeon, white and yellow perch.

There's a multitude of fine golf courses, all kinds of tennis courts, riding trails and swimming pools, and what is billed as the best hunting in the state—658 square miles of wilderness terrain open to the public.

There are more festivals in the Catskills than in any other section of the state, perhaps in the nation. Festivals celebrating the Irish, the Scots, the Germans, the Poles, the Indians; parades and youth fairs and a Country Music Festival with Nashville super stars. There's even a wine festival—this part of the Hudson Valley has been producing wine for over 150 years. But they could also have a maple syrup festival, because the country is the foremost producer in the eastern United States.

Hudson, in Columbia County, is the oldest city in the state, and its American Museum of Firefighting is worth the trip, with more than twenty-five pieces of equipment on display, dating from 1731 to 1900. In Athens, most of which is a Historic District, there's an interesting collection of eighteenth-century homes; in Coxsackie is the Bronck House Museum, one of the finest surviving examples of early Dutch design in the valley; in Catskill a group of activists are restoring the home of Thomas Cole, leader of the famed Hudson River school of painting; and on Route 9G, a mile from the Rip Van Winkle Bridge, is Olana, a castle that's Persian in design, built by Frederick Edwin Church, another member of the Hudson River school.

And then, of course, there are all those accommodations that are considered special enough to be included in this book.

Holistic Hideaway
UJJALA'S
New Paltz

Considering a diet? Deciding to make one final effort at getting your whole body in shape? Then search out this lilac Victorian house with striking Colonial-blue shutters and plum trim, tucked into a grove of pine and maple. Innkeeper Ujjala Schwartz, a dynamo of determination, will start you down the glory road of rejuvenation.

An expert in stress management and body therapy, a lecturer on holistics at the University College in New Paltz, and the coordinator of the Holistic Way Program at Mohonk Mountain House for three years, Ujjala will start you off with special diet foods, fresh vegetable juices, home-grown sprouts, and herbal teas, then take you through a session of shiatsu—deep relaxation massage.

But if you merely want to get away from it all, hiding in the woods in a 1910 Victorian home of captivating charm, breakfasting in a country kitchen or outdoors on the deck looking out at the apple, pear, and quince trees on Ujjala's 3½ acres, feasting on fresh fruits, eggs, omelets, pancakes, homemade breads, freshly ground coffee, and special teas, then this is the place.

The three rooms are individually decorated, and like Ujjala, they have great style. The downstairs room has its own skylight, leaded windows, a fireplace, and old barn siding; the two upstairs rooms are named Victorian and Country, one done in rose and light green, the other in blue and beige. Pillows, comforters, jugs, baskets of lace and dyed wools accessorize the accommodations most attractively.

Ujjala's is a non-Catskills kind of retreat, one that stands in total contrast to the town's Huguenot Street Historic District. The oldest street in America to retain its original houses, it was laid out by Huguenots, who had

60

Ujjala's

finally found a place of refuge after years of exile from their native France. They named the land purchased from the Esopus Indians *die Pfalz*, honoring the Rhine Palatinate where they had previously found temporary safety.

The oldest stone structures date from 1692, including the Jean Hasbrouck Memorial House, which has a steeply pitched roof typical of Northern European homes, and a jambless fireplace and gigantic chimney—it's one of the most outstanding examples of medieval Flemish stone architecture in the country.

Tours of that home and others commence at the Deyo Assembly Hall, which has a small gift shop, and the Howard Hasbrouck Grimm gallery and museum.

UJJALA's, 2 Forest Glen, New Paltz, New York 12561. Telephone: (914) 255-6360. Accommodations: three rooms with shared baths. Rates: moderate; includes full breakfast, afternoon tea. No cards. Pets not permitted. Open all year.

Getting There: Take Route 299 west from center of town to last traffic light. Then go south onto Route 208 for 3½ miles to Forest Glen Road on right. Ujjala's is first house on right.

A Pension in the Provinces

ASTORIA HOTEL
Rosendale

Nestled nicely between an outcropping of cliff and the Rondout Creek, in a valley where the mountains of the Catskill and Shawangunk ranges collide, this three-story stone structure squats ever so solidly on Main Street. This town was once crawling with miners who worked the ingredients for cement from surrounding hills and slopes—the cement in the century-old Brooklyn Bridge and in the nation's Capitol came from Rosendale. The Astoria, built in the early years of the Civil War, housed many of the miners, as well as travelers traversing the Delaware and the Hudson Canal.

Railroads, automobiles, and artificial cement meant demise and depression, but thanks to the energies and skills of Jeannine Gleissner, who started her restoration efforts in 1980, some of the town's past has been recreated. And more than a few touches of the French provinces have been added. The Astoria is now as much an auberge, or maybe a Parisian pension, as it is a hotel; for alongside is a ground-floor gourmet-to-go shop with tables and a fine line of imported cheeses and all kinds of sausages and cold cuts, with homemade salads, soups, and main dishes.

Jeannine's Gourmeteria is the perfect provider of picnic fare to take along when exploring the area. Begin by motoring north a dozen miles to Kingston, laid out as a Dutch village in the 1650s. The Kingston Stockade District today is based on a street plan that once contained the military stockade surveyed by Gov. Peter Stuyvesant. Along with the many pre-Revolutionary stone structures, there are Victorian and Greek Revival buildings and the most famous landmark in town, the Senate House, which is where the state's first constitution was announced and discussed in 1777. Refurbished by the state, the mansion has an adjacent museum with an art gallery featuring the landscapes and portraits of Kingston native John Vanderlyn, a noted nineteenth-century artist.

There are many other attractions in the area, including the Hurley Historic District two miles west of Kingston. It was originally named Nieuw Dorp by the Dutch, whose influence is still obvious, especially in such stone structures as the Hurley Patentee Manor, home of Colonial land agent Cornelius Cool, who built what is now a museum in 1696.

Jeannine will be happy to advise about other spots of interest, after guests have been awakened by that splendid breakfast centered around freshly baked baguettes and croissants, omelets, French toast, bacon, and other offerings.

The rooms and the hallway, with its fine railing saved from some other building slated for destruction, are comfortable, the beds are solid oak, the accessory pieces antique, and there's always a vase of fresh flowers in place.

ASTORIA HOTEL, 25 Main Street, Rosendale, New York 12472. Telephone: (914) 658-8201. Accommodations: eight rooms, each with private bath; no televisions or telephones; kitchenettes at extra charge. Rates: moderate; includes breakfast/brunch. No cards. Pets not permitted. Open all year.

Getting There: From New Paltz follow State Road 32 to Rosendale, turning left at State Road 213, which is Main Street and leads to High Falls; the inn is on the left side of the street.

CAPTAIN SCHOONMAKER'S HOUSE
High Falls

What do you get when you put a college professor, a grade school teacher, and a recent college graduate together in a historic home alongside a landmark canal? A country inn of class, of course. One with a dozen rooms filled with all kinds of in-tune period pieces, canopied and brass beds, fireplaces, and the friendliest level of hospitable innkeeping.

Sam Krieg is the professor, at the State University of New York in nearby New Paltz, Julia Krieg is the third-grade teacher in New Paltz, and daughter Julie is fresh out of college and now a successful entrepreneur with Julie's Ice Cream Parlor not far from the main house. That's the crew who took the grand old stone home of local patriot Capt. Frederick Schoonmaker and converted it to the happiest of hostelries, restoring a carriage house and a locktender's home on the Delaware-Hudson Canal and tending the eight acres of shaded garden and woods with great care.

Where the good captain used to provide refuge for those fleeing the ravages of the American Revolution, the Kriegs are now serving country breakfasts. They start off with a grapefruit-cranberry drink, or in season, a fresh strawberry compote, and continue with such specialties as a cheese-dill soufflé or a zucchini omelet with bits of crunchy bacon sprinkled on top, accompanied with fresh-baked breads spread with the Kriegs' own peach preserves and grape jelly. On some days Julia makes blueberry-coconut strudel, on others chocolate-apple-cinnamon cake.

Those breakfasts last the guests through most of the day, but in the hot summer season, what could be better later in the afternoon than some ice cream at Julie's Parlor, a beautifully restored antique building complete with a player piano and lots of enthusiastic country charm?

Captain Schoonmaker's House, built in 1760, is in very good hands.

CAPTAIN SCHOONMAKER'S HOUSE, Route 213, High Falls, New York 12440. Telephone: (914) 687-7946. Accommodations: 12 rooms sharing baths (one for each two rooms), some with television; no telephones; two rooms with working fireplaces. Rates: moderate, including full breakfast. No cards. Pets not permitted. Open all year.

Getting There: The inn is on the main road, State Road 213, which runs from High Falls and Rosendale.

DEPUY CANAL HOUSE
High Falls

Actually, there are two houses, the indestructible stone sentinel that used to watch over Lock 16 of the Delaware and Hudson Canal, and, across the street, the Brodhead House, named for the man who built the Italianate structure in 1869.

The Canal House was constructed of locally quarried stone and hand-hewn timbers by one Simeon DePuy in 1797 to serve as a hostelry for travelers along the Old Mine Road as well as the canal. Seventy years after that canal ceased operations, causing the tavern to close, a young chef named John Novi arrived on the scene with his mother. That was in 1964. The next five years were spent in the full-scale restoration of a building that was in serious need of rehabilitation.

By the middle of 1969 John opened phase one—his intimate little restaurant. Then lightning struck in the person of Craig Claiborne, who was overwhelmed by the food, to the point of awarding John's Canal House the coveted four stars.

John was then cooking on a simple little four-burner stove in a thimble of a kitchen, and he too was overwhelmed as the phone rang off the hook and Claiborne's readers arrived in droves.

John survived, and today his back room is considerably larger—guests are invited to come in and watch the action, or to use the phone: it's the only one in the building.

The Novi performance is still worthy of four stars. His presentation of fowl is fabulous—breasts of quail filled with venison quenelles lightly ladled with a dark mushroom sauce and presented in a nest of lavin, the very thin Japanese vermicelli noodles. Perfectly steamed asparagus spears lie alongside. A terrine of sole has a watercress-green center embraced by seaweed, crowned with a rose-sculpted tomato and covered with a heavenly coriander-coconut sauce.

At the house that John rebuilt, the glorious galantine of duckling is served with a lingonberry pudding, a lobster jambalaya includes mussels and chicken, and the smoked swordfish is delivered with creamed spinach.

They do their own smoking, as they do their own everything, including the blending of the lightest of dressings for the spinach-sweet onion salad, the preparation of such dessert delights as ricotta cheesecake with rhubarb-cream sauce, and English custard with a white-chocolate sabayon spiked with hazelnut liqueur.

All that plus impeccable service and two stories of history in an array of rooms filled with art and artifacts.

The wines at DePuy, which is open Thursday through Sunday for dinner only, are as beautifully selected and eclectic as the foods—there are labels from Australia, Idaho, Oregon as well as from the better-known vineyards of the world.

There's similar variety in the large yellow brick building across the way: Red, White, and Blue rooms, inspired only coincidentally by the Stars and Stripes. Well appointed, filled with fresh flowers every day, they are on the second floor, over an old-fashioned ice cream parlor.

DEPUY CANAL HOUSE, Route 213, High Falls, New York 12440. Telephone: (914) 687-7700/7777. Accommodations: three rooms with shared baths; no televisions or telephones. Rates: moderate; includes Continental breakfast. Cards: MC, V. Open all year except for a month in mid-January to mid-February; restaurant closed from mid-February through March.

Getting There: The inn is in the middle of the sleepy little crossroads of High Falls.

Art and Antiques

THE BAKERS
Stone Ridge

The charming information sheet put together by Doug and Fran Sutherland Baker advises that "Nearby you can bird, bicycle, hike, ski, snowshoe, fish, golf and play tennis. Watercolor instruction is available from your artist hostess . . . Looking forward to meeting you."

And they mean it. Doug is a biologist and a dedicated naturalist, Fran is the artist. Together they transformed a 1760 stone house into a happy haven, one sprinkled with antiques and cozy down comforters for those chilly evenings when the guests don't want to leave the living room fireplace.

There's another warming hearth in the dining room where the bountiful breakfasts are served: fresh baked breads, spinach or asparagus omelets, bacon, ham, sausage, and good coffee. There's also a breakfast nook in the solarium-greenhouse with its view of the mountains. On the Bakers' five acres one is always aware of those mountains, and the woods and fields. And the history. This Dutch Colonial reminder of the past is in the Rondout

Valley, the Rest Plaus, in Ulster, founded in 1664 and an important provider for the Continental Army during the Revolutionary War.

The Rondout Falls and Rondout River are close by, as is the Delaware and Hudson Canal Historical Society Museum, a late nineteenth-century Protestant church that now holds a collection of documents, maps, models and photographs of the canal that was once so crucial to the economy of the area.

For special dining experiences there's the DePuy Canal House and also Top of the Falls, with Mexican food on Wednesday, sushi and sashimi Thursday and Friday. Both places are in High Falls two miles down the road. For a real antiquing accommodation there are the two rooms on the top floor of the Banker's Daughter, a treasure trove of antiques on Route 209 in Stone Ridge (telephone 914-687-9088), run by the amiable Bonnie Salmon, a woman of infectious laughter, humor, and honesty.

THE BAKERS, R.D. 2 (P.O. Box 80), Old King's Highway, Stone Ridge, New York 12484. Telephone: (914) 687-9795. Accommodations: five rooms with two shared baths; no televisions or telephones, but television set in second-floor common area. Rates: moderate; includes full breakfast. No cards. Inquire about pets. Open all year.

Getting There: The inn is two miles from High Falls, south of the intersection of State Road 213 with 209.

Polish Provincial

COPPER HOOD INN
Allaben

In 1982 Helena from New Jersey and her partner from Queens took over a building housing a rather well-known French restaurant and a couple of dozen uninspired, rundown rooms. The industrious pair greased their elbows and went to it, scrubbing, painting, refurbishing, and furnishing, adding a huge indoor pool, a sauna, and a giant wooden deck all around the back of their inn, which is surrounded by its own twenty-seven-acre forest.

The rooms are functional and not at all fancy, and while the Continental cuisine which Polish-American Helena oversees may not measure up to the Gallic standards that once prevailed here, the aromas from the back room beckon and signal that the fare is solid and reliable.

Helena's orderly hostelry serves as a good, budget-minded base camp for partaking of all the pleasures of the Catskills: skiing, hiking, fishing, swimming, and oohing and aahing at the technicolor autumns during the annual losing of the leaves.

COPPER HOOD INN, Route 28, Allaben (post office address is Shandaken), New York 12480. Telephone: (914) 688-9962. Accommodations: 23 rooms, each with private bath; no televisions or telephones. Rates: inexpensive to moderate. Full meal and bar service. Children welcome; no pets. Cards: AE, CB, DC, MC, V. Open all year.

Getting There: The inn is at the crossroads known as Allaben, directly on State Road 28, two miles due east of Shandaken.

A Gallic Enclave

AUBERGE DES 4 SAISONS
Shandaken

Edouard and Annie Labeille are responsible for this slice of the French provinces tucked into a wooded slope of the Catskills, one that lives up fully to its 4 Saisons moniker. There is swimming, tennis, and croquet in the summer, skiing in the winter, hiking, leaf-watching, touring at any time of the year. And, always, guests can return to the glories of Gallic cuisine as interpreted by the tireless Edouard.

For three decades he's been pleasing guests with his special soups, brewed fresh daily to provide perfect preludes, whether he's blending a thick cream of cauliflower or carrot or avoiding the clichés of the usual crock and crust approach to French onion soup—he adds chunks of freshly chopped Swiss cheese to his version.

He's more traditional in his approach to snails, serving escargots, singing with the zing of garlic, in the shells with a standard snail holder provided. To give added oomph to the melon-prosciutto starter, he adds some strips of celeriac.

The steak Bercy, in a sauce made with meat glaze and showered with chopped shallots swimming in white wine, is splendid. Memorable meals also include roast lamb, a trio of thick slices delivered as precisely pink as ordered, bedded down with excellent roast potatoes and close-to-crunchy cauliflower.

Edouard's Napoleons are also in a special category, not as heavily layered as most, with custard that's not overly sweet. They are as good with the inn's strong coffee as their French bread is with the soup.

The dining room is simply furnished, the all-French wine list small but select, and there's a large redwood porch out front, christened Rendezvous Deck. It's an ideal staging area for pre- or post-prandial sipping, and for exchanging tall tales with other Auberge enthusiasts.

The deck is an integral part of the main inn building, which dates from 1870. It's where the simpler rooms are found. Across the courtyard, past the tennis courts, is a new addition, a motel-style unit designed to resemble a Swiss chalet. There all the rooms have private bath, private balconies or porches, and modest modern furnishings.

The favorite accommodation at this inn for all seasons is one of the second-floor chalet rooms with a balcony, and a favorite staffer is the ever-smiling Labeille granddaughter. A whiz of a waitress, she's a real asset to the Auberge.

AUBERGE DES 4 SAISONS, Route 42, Shandaken, New York 12480. Telephone: (914) 688-2223. Accommodations: 36 rooms, 17 with private bath; televisions but no telephones. Rates: inexpensive to moderate, modified American plan (breakfast and dinner). Full bar service. Children encouraged, but inquire about pets. Cards: AE, MC, V. Open all year except for a week during winter and the month of October.

Getting There: The Auberge is a mile north of the intersection of State Road 28 with State Road 42.

A Private Party

SHANDAKEN INN
Shandaken

Owners Albert and Gisele Pollack are not really interested in having the public swarm into their charming country inn cum 1880 dairy barn. They want to protect their privacy, to continue to keep it as it was when they first fled the city back in 1974 and bought this grand old vine-covered stone hideaway, eventually inviting a few friends to share their new-found retreat.

They are still inviting friends, and their friends' friends; but now they're charging them for the privilege of having a Continental breakfast and a banquet of a dinner: $150 a day per couple. One room with a large fireplace is $165 per day. If a full bar is desired, it's extra. And reservations are mandatory—even for friends—with bookings made far in advance.

The Shandaken is open only on weekends. That's when Gisele displays her many talents—as a superior chef whose French provincial origins are apparent with every forkful, as a gracious hostess, and as an interior designer of great taste. The antique-filled main room fanning out from a large, inviting fireplace is dotted with accent pieces, handsome couches, and deep-cushioned chairs, providing a warm setting for the few—a maximum of two dozen—friends/guests fortunate enough to be admitted into the inner circle presided over by handsome host Albert. It's a weekend indulgence in all that's good-looking and good cooking.

There's a pool and a tennis court on the premises, and, of course, all the nearby activities of the Catskills, so close to the hustle of the city, and yet so very, very far.

SHANDAKEN INN, Golf Course Road/Route 28, Shandaken, New York 12480. Telephone: (914) 688-5100. Accommodations: 12 rooms, each with private bath; no televisions or telephones. Rates: expensive. No children permitted. Inquire about small pets. No cards. Open weekends (Friday and Saturday nights) all year except April and November.

Getting There: The inn is 29 miles on State Road 28 from the Kingston Exit of the New York Thruway, nine-tenths of a mile from the junction of 28 with Route 42.

A Swinging Ski Lodge

GREENE MOUNTAIN VIEW INN
Tannersville

A few hundred yards from the main thoroughfare of State Road 23A, which bisects this sometimes sleepy crossroads, is this simple little hideaway with a fully stocked bar. When there's snow on the slope, Tannersville explodes with parkas, poles, and ski boots, and the Greene Mountain is usually filled with skiers and swingles. There's a game room for the younger set.

The modestly priced nightly buffets are great for big eaters, and in the mornings there are do-it-yourself Continental breakfasts, including a choice of cereals.

Owner Ray Tempo, an outgoing, genial innkeeper, recently modernized the rooms, installing cable television, upgrading bathrooms, and adding air conditioning for those months when the sun outshines the snow.

GREENE MOUNTAIN VIEW INN, Church and South Main streets (P.O. Box 710), Tannersville, New York 12485. Telephone: (518) 589-5511. Accommodations: 23 rooms, each with private bath; television; no telephones. Rates: inexpensive; includes Continental breakfast. Children welcome; no pets. Cards: MC, V. Open all year.

Getting There: Tannersville is in the northern heart of Catskill skiing country; the inn is two blocks from 23A.

No Nightmares Here

MARIE'S DREAM HOUSE
West Kill

For a money-saving trip to the Austrian Alps, climb fifteen hundred feet into the Northern Catskills and search out Austrian-born Marie Anders, who provides liberal batches of old world hospitality in her tidily appointed inn and restaurant. In the summer season her Viennese Pastry Garden is a magnet for all those who have forked their way through a Sachertorte at the source, those who could never say "no" to *doppelt schlag*, another dollop of rich whipped cream.

In colder times, cross-country skiers push off from the back door, and the downhill racers head for the mountains of Belair, Windham, and Hunter; the latter calls itself "The Snowmaking Capitol of the World," with an "o" in Capitol! There are actually three mountains at 4,025-foot-high

71

Marie's Dream House

Hunter, some thirty-two miles of skiable terrain, three lodges, a noted ski school, a fully stocked ski shop, a cafeteria, snack and pizza bars, a mini-deli, seven lifts and tows including a T-bar, a Poma lift, and four double chair lifts.

In summer, when Marie is getting superlatives for her strudel, Hunter hosts a cornucopia of special events, starting in early July with the Italian Festival and German Alps Festival. That's followed by the National Polka Festival, the Country Music Festival, the International Celtic Festival, and, finally, the Mountain Eagle American Indian Festival.

The German Alps Festival should appeal to the guests who like to gorge themselves on Marie's All You Care to Eat dinners, headlined with super home-brewed soups, slice after slice of gravy-coated sauerbraten, rouladen that Emperor Franz Josef would have applauded, and all kinds of schnitzels, followed, of course, by freshly baked pastry and lots of strong coffee.

There's beer and wine in Marie's Bar, and comfortable beds for resting after all that food—resting and looking out of the windows, sitting on the balcony, inhaling the good air of the mountains.

MARIE'S DREAM HOUSE, Route 42, West Kill, New York 12492. Telephone: (518) 989-6565. Accommodations: 16 rooms, each with private bath; no televisions or telephones. Rates: moderate; includes full breakfast. No cards. Inquire about pets. Open all year.

Getting There: The inn is on State Road 42 seven miles north of the junction with State Road 28 at Shandaken.

The British Are Coming!

THE REDCOAT'S RETURN
Elka Park

A few minutes from the informal simplicity of such accommodations as the Greene Mountain View Inn in Tannersville is this ultra-sophisticated slice of something very, very special and veddy, veddy British.

A country inn with great class, a four-story, gabled wooden frame structure originally built in 1910 to serve as one of the then-popular summer boardinghouses, it now serves as a mini-museum for the antiques and books gathered by owners Tom and Peggy Wright. He's British; she's American. Thus the name, and the wonderful sign out front depicting the pair, one in the obligatory redcoat, one in Colonial gown.

What a happy twosome they make as they move into their second decade of innkeeping, Peggy ever bubbling behind the cozy bar in the pub with its cheerful fireplace; Tom out back behind the burners churning out the kind of non-pub grub he learned to prepare while apprenticing at London's Dorchester and as chef on board the *Queen Mary*. And that means roast beef and Yorkshire pudding, of course, and steak and kidney pie, but also seafood—and while he can't really deliver fresh Dover sole, he does do wonders with the harvest from the American side of the deep. His dining room is open to the general public, and he's therefore able to maintain a sufficient volume to guarantee a regular supply of prime provisions.

In the mornings, inn guests are treated to a full-scale English country breakfast, featuring all kinds of English preserves and freshly baked rolls and muffins. Guests also receive a glass of sherry on arrival in their rooms, which are simply furnished in a period style. The Wrights will happily guide their guests to some of the neighboring reasons for staying with them: Schoharie Creek for trout fishing, the adjoining Catskill Game Preserve with hiking trails leading through the 250,000 acres roller-coasting up and down the hills and mountains, and the golf courses, the tennis courts, and the lakes for swimming. From the 3810-foot prominence of Sugarloaf Mountain, there's a breathtaking panorama of the Hudson Valley.

The indolent and the self-indulgent can stay on campus, lounging and reading on the porch resplendent with hanging pots of geraniums; and there's nothing cozier on a cold winter's day than cuddling into a couch with one of the Wrights' many books, in front of the fireplace with its moosehead gazing over this happy little empire.

THE REDCOAT'S RETURN, Dale Lane off Platte Clove Road, Elka Park, New York 12427. Telephone: (518) 589-6379/9858. Accommodations: 14 rooms, seven with private bath; no televisions or telephones; television in sitting room. Rates: moderate; includes full breakfast. Full bar service. Children welcome; no pets. Cards: AE, MC, V. Closed April, May, and first three weeks of November, with a two-night minimum stay required on winter weekends and three nights on holiday weekends.

Getting There: From the town of Tannersville drive 4½ miles south on County Road 16 to Dale Lane and the sign for the inn.

74

A Catskill Semi-Classic
WINTER CLOVE INN
Round Top

For a century and a half the Whitcomb family has been welcoming guests to this haven of congeniality nestled in a peaceful valley on the northern slope of the Catskills. That means five generations of providing year-round country hospitality and solid fare three times a day for their guests: those who walk the links on the inn's nine-hole golf course or work on their backhand on the tennis and badminton courts, splash in the indoor and outdoor pools, test their bowling skills, or hike the many trails on the grounds and throughout the adjacent Catskill Mountain Forest Preserve.

In the snowy season the inn lives up to its name as guests don ice skates and skis. Two hundred years ago surveyors in the area christened the place when they found snow and ice delaying the arrival of spring in the valley, then known as a *clove*.

The inn's easy-to-follow trail map portrays the pawprints of the creatures that roam these wilds as well as the leaf configurations of the trees: hickory and sugar maple, ash and oak, poplar and yellow birch. There are trails for all levels of hikers, including those who want to ascend to the

summit of North Mountain to join the New York State Trail System or proceed to Rip's Rock overlooking Rip Van Winkle Hollow and the Hudson River. En route are stone quarries, charcoal pits, stone walls, and logging roads, and the ruins of the once famous Catskill Mountain House, a grand hotel of the nineteenth century. The inn packs picnic lunches, but for those who want to live off the land, there's a wonderful bakery run by a German-Polish couple in Round Top, not far from the inn—Hartmann's Kaffeehaus. They serve breakfast, sandwiches, superlative fruit tarts, and walnut and coconut squares that are impossible to resist.

When you return to the inn after a day's outing, you return to mountain heaven Catskill style, with rockers on the porch for just a-sittin' and a-rockin' and visitin'. When the Winter Clove earns its name, the guests gather before the stone fireplace.

WINTER CLOVE INN, Winter Clove Road (P.O. Box 67), Round Top, New York 12473. Telephone: (518) 622-3267. Accommodations: 35 rooms in the main inn, 15 in the cottage units, each with private bath; no televisions or telephones; television in lounge. Rates: moderate; American plan. Pets not permitted. Cards: MC, V. Open all year.

Getting There: 1.6 miles from County Road 31 (Heart's Content Road!) in Round Top, turn at Winter Clove Road, following the markers at all crossroads. The inn is at the end of the road at the top of the hill, just past Pickwick Lodge.

Arms and the Women (and Apologies to G. B. Shaw)
GREENVILLE ARMS
Greenville

Barbara and Laura Stevens are the affable innkeepers of this Victorian three-story mansion, replete with turret and bay window and double-decker porch. It dominates a seven-acre spread with a carefully tended, quiet little garden and a pair of little bridges spanning a brook and leading to a separate carriage house at the rear of the property, one with nine rooms and a common television/living room. The room called Haymow, number 18, is a favorite because it has a second-floor private porch.

In addition to a fine swimming pool, there are also croquet, shuffleboard, badminton and volleyball courts on the grounds, and also an adequate supply of lawn chairs for the less athletically inclined.

The Stevens sisters know their house well: their mother bought it in the 1950s and they grew up there. When she died in 1981 the pair took over

76

Greenville Arms

the reins, running the same kind of orderly, well-maintained operation. That means dinners promptly at 6:00 pm (1:00 pm on Sundays) and following a set routine; baked fish on Friday, turkey on the weekends, baked chicken, ham, stuffed pork chops on other nights, and always fresh-baked breads, cakes, and pies.

Meals, including a hearty breakfast, are served in a grand old high-ceilinged dining room with polished woods, mantelpieces of oak, and a scattering of Victorian period pieces. The guest rooms also evoke the spirit of the past, in the main building where front rooms have access to that grand porch, a fine place for contemplating the quiet of this hideaway in the foothills of the Catskills.

Built in the 1890s by William Vanderbilt, it's one of the few remaining reminders of those glorious free-spending days of the Gilded Age.

GREENVILLE ARMS, Greenville, New York 12083. Telephone: (518) 966-5219. Accommodations: 20 rooms, 9 in carriage house with private bath, 11 in main house, 5 with private bath; telephones but no televisions. Rates: moderate; modified American plan. No bar service. No cards. Pets not permitted. Open May–November.

Getting There: At the intersection of State Roads 81 and 32 in Greenville, go south on 32; the inn is the second house on the right.

SARATOGA
ADIRONDACKS
CENTRAL NEW YORK

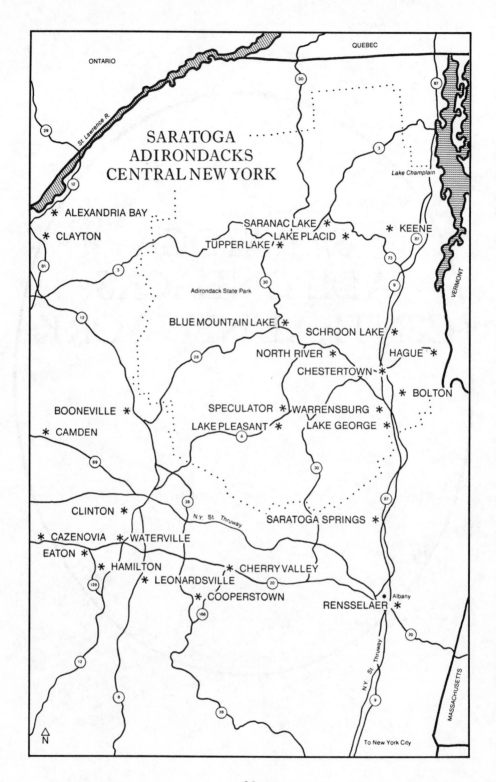

SARATOGA
ADIRONDACKS
CENTRAL NEW YORK

ONTARIO

QUEBEC

St. Lawrence R.

Lake Champlain

* ALEXANDRIA BAY

* CLAYTON

SARANAC LAKE *
LAKE PLACID *

* KEENE

TUPPER LAKE *

Adirondack State Park

BLUE MOUNTAIN LAKE *

SCHROON LAKE *

NORTH RIVER *

HAGUE *

CHESTERTOWN *

* BOLTON

* BOONEVILLE

SPECULATOR * * WARRENSBURG

* CAMDEN

LAKE PLEASANT * * LAKE GEORGE *

VERMONT

CLINTON *

N.Y. St. Thruway

SARATOGA SPRINGS *

* CAZENOVIA * WATERVILLE

EATON *

* HAMILTON

* LEONARDSVILLE

* CHERRY VALLEY

* COOPERSTOWN

Albany

RENSSELAER *

N.Y. St. Thruway

MASSACHUSETTS

To New York City

N

SARATOGA

SARATOGA SPRINGS AREA

Three hours from the middle of Manhattan and a half hour from the state capital is a full-scale retreat into yesterday known as Saratoga Springs. It was America's first full-blown red-white-and-blue resort, the queen of spas. Today it's a picture-postcard assemblage of Victorian and Edwardian architecture in the foothills of the Adirondacks, a year-round escape with something for everyone, the birthplace of thoroughbred racing in the United States.

The first jockeys rode their charges around a local track in 1863, and the following year the Saratoga Race Course was opened. Today the ponies do their pounding for twenty-four days in late July and August, and early-morning breakfasts at the track are still the best way to get into the spirit of the sport of kings. For the history of it, visit Saratoga's National Museum of Thoroughbred Racing with its jockeys' Hall of Fame, its colorful collection of racing silks, its array of equine art, and its fine Peale portrait of George Washington.

Standardbreds go through their paces at the Saratoga Harness Raceway from April to November and on weekends January through March. There's also world-class polo in August.

For the non-horsy set, there's the Ann Grey Art Gallery rambling through the Casino, an 1870 three-story Italianate mansion with seven rooms furnished in the kind of damn-the-expense style that typified the Gilded Age. Pick up a flyer detailing self-guided tours at the Casino or at the little information booth on the town's main road. Also, study the schedule of the Saratoga Performing Arts Center, a $4 million stunner with covered seating for 5,100 and space for another 20,000 on the grassy plains of the heavily wooded Spa State Park.

There's plenty of window-shopping on the main streets of Saratoga, and bibliophiles will be stunned by an old- and rare-book store in the center of town. Skidmore College makes its own special contribution to this beautiful blend of the old and the new, and it's still possible to take the waters here, at the state-run spa. In private chambers one is immersed, tickled by millions of tiny carbonated bubbles, then massaged for twenty minutes and layered with hot sheets for another thirty.

There are other spas in this city of springs, and you may find them essential if you visit in the winter and overdo while skiing on the slopes and cross-country trails, ice skating at the city rink, or pulling a big one out of the frozen lake.

Some form of exercise is necessary for those who over-indulge at Saratoga's finer eating establishments. At Mrs. London's Bake Shop and Café, 33 Philadelphia Street, for example, your eyes will be opened by a breakfast of French toast made from brioche bread and served with grilled Black Forest ham and pure maple syrup. The pâtisserie-cafe is not quite as good as when Craig Claiborne discovered it two years ago—their coffee cakes tasted at least two days old when we breakfasted there—but they still have good sourdough and such blah-breaking snacks as smoked chicken salad, and smoked mozzarella tangled with roasted red peppers, black olives, tomatoes, and fresh basil.

C'est Cheese at 404 Broadway is an open-daily gourmeteria loyal to its name, and the Olde Bryan Inn at 123 Maple Avenue is faithful to its title: it's the oldest structure in town (1773), a wide-beamed stone-walled tavern with three fireplaces and an all-day menu of salads and sandwiches, all kinds of omelets and burgers. The Spa Brauhaus on East High Street at the Ballston Spa is the place for schnitzels and sauerbraten, and Chez Sophie at 69 Caroline is a prix-fixe joy forever, an artistically appointed converted home with a split personality—brick and wood up front by the splendid bar, lacy Victorian out back with an air of formality. Everywhere the artistic achievements of Joseph C. Parker strike the eye and stimulate the spirit.

Meryl Streep was Sophie's Choice but Joe Parker has the choice Sophie—she's his wife and a whiz in the kitchen—and together they run a class act. They also have a class daughter, one who played the teacher in *Kramer vs. Kramer*, and Ethel Kennedy on the TV series.

Her rave reviews are posted for guests chez Sophie to read while awaiting such Sophie sensations as duckling enhanced with apricot and pink peppercorn sauce, veal in a velvety cream sauce, and freshly made sorbets. A final plus: Sophie, once ranked the seventh best woman fencer in the world, maintains the neatest kitchen in the state.

Button-in-a-Banister Heirloom

TIBBITTS' HOUSE INN
Rensselaer

Built in the decade before the Civil War alongside a trail blazed by General Knox during the Revolutionary War, this lovingly tended highway hugger has been in the same family for well over half a century. Innkeeper Claire Rufleth narrates its history with pride—her grandfather built the wraparound porch with its fine oak wainscoting, all eighty-four feet of it, and the old-fashioned porch swing in a corner is the same one she sat in as a child. Husband Herb can tell you about the ivory mortgage button embedded in the newel post at the base of the walnut banister—when they found it in an antique store years ago, they thought the $19 price tag a bit excessive, but they just had to have it. Through the years they've found other antiques to add to the special ambience of their inn.

The grounds are well manicured and bright with blooms all summer, and one would have to search far and wide to find an accommodation as cozy as the old Keeping Room, with its corner raised-hearth fireplace and original beam ceiling.

For a small extra charge the Rufleths serve their "Hudson River Valley Breakfast," a real belt-buster with all the trimmings, and they'll be happy to point out directions to local sights and sites.

Close by is Fort Crailo, established by the Dutch Rensselaers in about 1700 and open today as a museum which offers many insights into the lifestyles of the Dutch pioneers who were so important in these parts. Tradition has it that a British surgeon wrote "Yankee Doodle" at the fort in 1758.

A couple of miles from the inn there's a forty-five-mile paved path that parallels the Hudson, and across the river is Albany, second-oldest permanent settlement in the thirteen colonies. Among its many attractions are the 1881 Richardson-designed City Hall and the Governor Nelson A. Rockefeller Empire State Plaza, a ninety-six-acre, $2 billion complex with art gallery and theaters. In the New York State Museum there are many life-sized dioramas and vividly arranged exhibits detailing the development of the state. And be sure to see the 1715 St. Peter's Episcopal Church and the century-old Capitol with its incredible staircase and beautiful gardens. Also worth a visit are two mansions, one an elegant expression of Georgian style, named for Gen. Philip Schuyler, and one named for Gen. Abraham Ten Broeck. Cherry Hill presents the chronology of the Van Rensselaers, who lived in the home through two hundred years.

83

TIBBITTS' HOUSE INN, 100 Columbia Turnpike (State Roads 9 and 20) Clinton Heights, Rensselaer, New York 12144. Telephone: (518) 472-1348. Accommodations: five rooms, three doubles and two singles with shared baths; no televisions or telephones. Rates: inexpensive. No cards. Children not permitted; no pets. Open all year.

Getting There: Take route 787 North from the Thruway and drive 4 miles east on routes 9 and 20 to the inn.

The Past Prevails
THE GIDEON PUTNAM
Saratoga Springs

It's not a cozy little country inn. The Gideon Putnam, named for the town's first promoter-developer, is the ultimate expression of Victorian elegance, a vibrant echo of Saratoga Springs' golden age, a time when private railroad cars whisked the wealthy to the spa to play the horses and take the waters.

Three-story, eggshell-white Corinthian columns and an oversized green canopy greet guests under giant oaks. There's no less eye-pleasing pleasure in the lobby, with marble and mirrors and cheery fireplaces, and well-appointed patios fanning out beyond the French doors.

In summer months there's a well-stocked lunch wagon for fine front porch munching and special libations of the day for those resting between sets of tennis on the eight clay courts, or rounds of golf on the hotel's two courses, or some strenuous swimming in a monster of a Victorian pool. Numerous trails lead off to the woods, to the waters, to the Performing Arts Center; there are seemingly unlimited picnic possibilities on the fifteen hundred acres of Saratoga State Park, and bikes are available to rent.

The formal Georgian dining room, where wall murals, soft music, and candlelight melt into a marvelous mood, is as appealing as the upper-floor suites with their adjoining wicker-filled porches. Avoid the fifth floor, which has been "motelized" in a mistaken fit of modernity; the other rooms manage to maintain the air of a lost and more leisurely paced time.

The Sunday brunch is outstanding and the desserts would satisfy an Orson Welles—or maybe a William Howard Taft—and the special Champagne Weekend package deals just might be "The Most Romantic Weekend in America," as management boasts.

THE GIDEON PUTNAM, Saratoga Springs, New York 12866. Telephone: (518) 584-3000. Accommodations: 132 rooms and suites, each with private bath, telephone, and television. Full meal and bar service. Rates:

The Gideon Putnam

expensive, especially in summer; full American plan available. Cards: AE, CB, DC, MC, V. Pets not permitted. Open all year.

Getting There: From the center of town follow U.S. 9, South Broadway Street, south to the Spa State Park and follow Avenue of Pines directly to the hotel.

Kick Up Your Heels in Victoriana
ADELPHI HOTEL
Saratoga Springs

Smack in the center of Saratoga Springs' elegant blend of old and new is this 1877 Italianate marvel with fabulous fretwork on the facade, a graceful "Saratoga Porch," a grand circus-sized lobby, and enough ferns, ceiling fans, and cut glass to make one wonder if Lillian Russell and Diamond Jim are not lurking around the corner.

The registration desk is easily one of the most dramatic of all the inns in this guide, and the indoor-outdoor dining areas are among the most appealing. Start your time-capsule trip into yesterday with a stop at the Victorian Bar, topping off a splash of Campari or Pernod with Saratoga water, then enter the Saratoga Club and go Continental with escargots in puff pastry with a lightly garlicked cream sauce. Or fork into a robust pâté, some baked marinated French goat cheese, or a smoked chicken breast saluted with chopped walnuts and set awash in herbed walnut oil vinaigrette. Soft-shell crabs, complemented by a light Provençal tomato sauce bristling with fresh basil and thyme, is a summer specialty of the house; but the charcoal-grilled fresh salmon, the roast duck in a black currant sauce, and the fettuccine tossed with scallions, shallots, and tomatoes sautéed in vodka are also something special.

And when you're finished feasting, you can kick up your heels in a high-ceilinged room with furnishings reflecting the lifestyles of a century ago. Other rooms are vintage 1920s, reflecting an earlier renovation.

ADELPHI HOTEL, 365 Broadway, Saratoga Springs, New York 12866. Telephone: (518) 587-4688. Accommodations: 20 rooms and suites, each with private bath and telephone. Full bar service. Lunch and dinner served only in July and August. Rates: moderate to expensive, including Continental breakfast; two-night minimum required on holidays and weekends during racing season. Cards: AE, MC, V. Pets not permitted. Open May through November.

Getting There: The Adelphi is in the center of town, on the main street, Broadway, which is also U.S. 9.

Cozy and Clean

THE KIMBERLY
Saratoga Springs

Close to all the in-town action, just three blocks from the Casino and its Congress Park, is this century-old guest house, the only one in town that never closes its doors. It's a prim and proper white storybook-variety two-level cottage, with Victorian gables and a latticework entry canopy. Outdoor tables and chairs are strategically situated on the lawn with its carefully tended flower beds, and everywhere there are signs that the owner, Ingrid Downie, who lives on the premises, cares about her guests and their creature comforts. She also cares about their travel budgets. Most of the rooms have a small kitchenette; a few have hot plates and refrigerators.

THE KIMBERLY, 158 South Broadway, Saratoga Springs, New York 12866. Telephone: (518) 584-9006. Accommodations: 8 rooms, 6 with private bath, all with television but no telephones. Rates: inexpensive. No cards. Open all year.

Getting There: The Kimberly is in the center of town, on the corner of Broadway and Lincoln Avenue.

Simple Summer Setting
WASHINGTON INN
Saratoga Springs

Close to the Washington and Lincoln Baths in Saratoga Spa Park stands this double-decker, ole-timey structure with a variety of accommodations to suit families of all sizes and shapes. And many families keep returning year after year to this place, which has been in the same family for several generations. Today it is painted the same shade of green that used to dominate the summer camp landscape in the 1940s. The woman in charge is an amiable, chatty soul who's always willing to point out local attractions and sites of interest, and she oversees a staff that renders a high level of maintenance in the rooms. The grounds are great for stretching young and old muscles alike, and abutting are the hundreds of acres of park.

WASHINGTON INN, South Broadway Street, Saratoga Springs, New York 12866. Telephone: (518) 584-9807. Accommodations: 20 rooms, each with private bath, two with kitchenettes; no televisions or telephones. Rates: inexpensive to moderate; one-week minimum stay during racing season. No cards. Children accepted. Well-trained pets permitted. Open July through August.

ADIRONDACKS

THE ADIRONDACKS

What do you get when you put together the national parks of Olympic, Glacier, Yellowstone, and Yosemite?

The Adirondack State Park—almost. The 9,000 square miles of forest, interlaced with 30,000 miles of clear rivers and streams splashing into another 1,000 miles of river, is larger than all of those national parks combined. It's a state-guaranteed "forever wild" haven for the harried, and home of the world's oldest mountains—once loftier than the Rockies but now glacier-ground into more manageable sizes. There are still forty-six peaks over four thousand feet high.

Larger than the state of Massachusetts and sparkling with Lakes George, Champlain, Tupper, and Upper and Lower Saranac, the park and its adjacent lands have something for everyone, from mountains for climbers and hikers, to innumerable ribbons of water for anglers seeking trout, bass, pike, and landlocked salmon. There are rugged lodges, dude ranches, campgrounds galore, pampering inns echoing with the good-life reminders of an earlier era, some surviving Great Camps built by the super rich, and a good many summer camps for kids from all economic backgrounds.

There are the legends of the Winter Olympics at Lake Placid, the Coney Island atmosphere of some of the Lake George area, canoeing challenges—especially the eighty-six-mile trip through the Fulton Chain of Lakes—and whitewater rafting; but above all, there are places to find solace and solitude.

For the more culturally inclined, there's a superb Adirondack Museum at Blue Mountain Lake, open from 10 to 6 daily from mid-June to mid-October (telephone 518-352-7311)—a collection of eighteen buildings on thirty acres illustrating in vivid manner the lifestyles of an earlier time. The artisans and craftsmen are honored, as are those artists who captured the glories of Adirondack country on canvas: Winslow Homer, Thomas Cole, Homer Martin, and A. F. Tait.

Also at Blue Mountain Lake is the Adirondack Lakes Center for the Arts, a July to August staging area for concerts and films, art shows, dramas and musicals, arts and crafts instruction. For a current schedule telephone (518) 352-7715.

At Elizabethtown there's the Essex County Historical Society's Adirondack Center Museum, open May 15 through October 15 from 9 to 5 Monday–Saturday and from 1 to 5 on Sundays. It too provides insights into early life in the area, with antique home and farm furnishings and implements and a second-floor Adirondack Inn exhibit showing how tourists were treated in the 1880s. There are old dolls and toys, a collection of paintings, a carefully manicured Colonial garden, and an old schoolroom, complete with a dunce stool for sitting in the corner.

Ann's Finest Hour

BLENHEIM ON THE LAKE
Lake George

When Ann deAvila was bitten by the innkeeping bug, husband Rolando blessed her enthusiasm and determination with a "Full speed ahead." "It's safer than a red sports car and less dangerous than having an affair," the affable Ann trilled when we happened across this grand old lakefront mansion named for Winston Churchill's famous country estate. "Call it mid-life crisis; call it madness, but I love it!" Together with her sons and daughters, Ann is working a gradual transformation of the sixteen-bedroom stone house built in 1895 for one Royal C. Peabody, a utilities magnate who founded Brooklyn Edison.

The first conversion was in the basement—a space now known as Churchill's Pub—and it looks over the northern shores of the thirty-two-mile-long Lake George, a bustler of a place in most of its parts, with string after string of fast feeders and plastic motels.

But at Blenheim Ann is providing a happy alternative, declaring her independence from such dissonance. Working carefully and at a high level of luxurious taste, she has converted five of the large and high-ceilinged rooms into something special, with tile fireplaces, carved stair railings, leaded and stained-glass windows, wide halls, and gargantuan bathrooms with giant shower stalls and tubs. Wallpaper and towels are carefully color coordinated, and there's a common room on the second floor for meeting other guests happy to escape Lake George realities. The two-bedroom suite overlooking the lake is ideal for a couple with a child.

BLENHEIM ON THE LAKE, Route 9N (P.O. Box 429), Lake Shore Drive, Lake George, New York 12845. Telephone: (518) 668-5580. Accommodations: 5 rooms, each with private bath; no televisions or telephones. Rates: moderate; includes Continental breakfast. Cards: AE, MC, V. Pets not permitted. Open mid-June to Labor Day.

Getting There: Take Exit 22 off of Northway, then drive north on Lake Shore Drive to the inn's large sign.

When Is a Motel Not a Motel?

DUNHAM'S BAY LODGE
Lake George

Without doubt this is one of the most fussily maintained facilities to be found anywhere along the 109 miles of four-season fun and sport known as the Lake George shoreline. Dunham's Bay Lodge fronts on a marina and boasts its own sandy beach, spacious lawns, and a variety of accommodations, including cabins with fireplaces.

Comfortably tucked into a secluded bay just a few miles from all the action in Lake George Village, it's ably run by John and Kathy Salvador, innkeepers who are proud of their Swiss chalet with its individually decorated bedrooms and its nightly movies. The lodge is a good base camp for exploring some of the history of the area—and there's a fair share of it, despite all the motel modernity.

Fort William Henry is a few miles south, and if you know your James Fenimore Cooper you know it was built in the middle of the eighteenth century during the French and Indian War. It's been painstakingly restored, utilizing the original plans. Hundreds of Colonial and Indian artifacts, unearthed during the reconstruction, are on display, along with weapons of the era. There are interesting demonstrations of bullet-molding and musket and cannon firing by the State 1755 Acting Company, which moves through its military motions with great gusto.

In colder months there's the annual Winter Carnival Festival, held every weekend during February, with numerous competitions and contests including ice fishing. And for the hardy, there's the Polar Bear Swim Club.

DUNHAM'S BAY LODGE, Route 9L (R.D. 1, P.O. Box 111A), Lake George, New York 12845. Telephone: (518) 656-9242. Accommodations: 23 rooms, each with private bath and television, no telephones. Full meal and bar service. Rates: moderate. Cards: AE, MC, V. Pets not permitted. Open all year.

Getting There: From the Northway, I87, take exit 21 and drive north a half mile on State Road 9N, then turn right on 9L which leads directly to the inn.

AAAA (Artistic Achievement in Adirondacks Antique Capital)

MERRILL MAGEE HOUSE
Warrensburg

The Carrington clan are responsible for this Four-A achievement, a little jewel box in the heart of the self-proclaimed antiques center of the Adirondacks. There's Florence, Ken, and daughter Pam, who performs minor kitchen miracles, such as making an incredibly good strawberry pie. Her mud pie with coffee ice cream, is also in the prize-winning category, as is her fresh-baked nut bread and her baking powder biscuits.

Beef Wellington, duckling, tournedos, and New York strip steaks are regulars on Pam's select menu, and she always makes sure she has a supply of fresh vegetables in the larder. The choice depends on her success in the markets that day.

Pam also oversees a midday menu and the always-available Tavern's Ploughman's Lunch, as well as afternoon tea. Both, the Carringtons are proud to point out, reflect their own English heritage as well as that of the family that originally built the nineteenth-century pillared home with its Greek Revival facade.

A splendid little screened porch for al fresco feasting overlooks a well-manicured garden and pool. The pair of interior dining rooms are small and warmly appointed, with deep peach-colored carpeting, and stenciling on the walls softly illuminated by candlelight. The pine and pewter lounge that adjoins is another touch of England, but more country tavern in inspiration than pub. The fireplace crackles a warm welcome in the colder months.

But at any time of the year the Merrill Magee is a gem of a retreat, whether you've been schussing the slopes of nearby Gore Mountain—the Carringtons can arrange ski rentals—or browsing among the antiques. Gore is one of New York's greatest ski centers, with five chair lifts, J- and T-bars, and the state's only gondola.

The upstairs guest rooms are quaint, sparkling clean, and appointed with carefully selected antiques. Don't miss the bit of fun that surprises guests in the downstairs women's room.

MERRILL MAGEE HOUSE, Warrensburg, New York 12885. Telephone: (518) 623-2449. Accommodations: three rooms sharing a bath; no

Merrill Magee House

televisions or telephones. Rates: inexpensive; includes breakfast. Cards: AE, MC, V. Pets not permitted. Open all year.

Getting There: Warrensburg is off Exit 23 of Interstate 87, and the inn is in the center of town across from the small park and bandstand.

Hudson River Hideaway

COUNTRY ROAD LODGE
Warrensburg

Occupying a pinch of land alongside the rocky stream that passes for the Hudson River in these parts, this red-shingled country cottage ringed by the mountains is a perfect headquarters for summer hikers and berry pickers and for winter cross-country skiers.

Innkeeper Steve Parisi, native of the area and an emigré from Madison Avenue, likes his privacy. There's nothing in sight but mountains, the stream, an old railroad trestle bridge, a distant barn and silo. He also likes his gardening—he tends everything from lilacs to raspberries.

Convenient to Hickory Hill with its challenging twelve-hundred-foot vertical run and not far from two other ski centers, the lodge is surrounded by mile after mile of cross-country trails.

It's a strictly informal base camp, one with a common room sporting an upright piano, a wood-burning stove, and books and games.

During the summer season, Continental breakfast is included in the rates, and Steve, an able chef, will prepare for a reasonable fee something more elaborate, with homemade breads and maple syrup that is the real thing. But if you're looking for a bit of history with your food, don't miss the Grist Mill on River Street in town. Dating from 1824, it has a romantically cozy ground floor bar and lounge and an outdoor upstairs porch for airy repasts overlooking the Schroon River. Expert chef Bill Steele assembles the mightiest chef's salad in the state, and he does nice things to veal and then finishes you off with the richest of cakes.

COUNTRY ROAD LODGE, 12 Hickory Hill Road, Warrensburg, New York 12885. Telephone: (518) 623-2207. Accommodations: five rooms sharing two baths; no televisions or telephones. Rates: inexpensive; modified American plan in winter. No cards. Children accepted only when part of a group of eight. Pets not permitted. Open all year.

Getting There: From Main Street, State Road 9, take State Road 418 (opposite the stone church) three miles to Hickory Hill Road (where there's a sign for the Hickory Ski Center) and turn left, driving up a dirt road and into the pine forest for a half mile to the lodge.

Home on the Lake
THE HAYES HOUSE
Bolton Landing

The Hayes House is a Cape Cod cottage from the 1920s, nestled in the woods along a small slope of Adirondack wilderness on the shores of Lake George. It's one of the warmest home-away-from-homes in this book. The walls are pine-paneled, and one of the guest rooms has a delightful canopied double bed. Each of the rooms has its own private entrance; two of them have large screened porches overlooking the beauties of Green Island Bay, and there's a common room for television watching.

The beach is only a few feet away, tennis courts and restaurants are within easy walking distance, and up the hill a bit there's a five-mile-trail across Tongue Mountain. The Hayes family can arrange various boat tours, provide picnic lunches, and advise on what else to see and do in the area.

THE HAYES HOUSE, 7161 Lakeshore Drive, Bolton Landing, New York 12814. Telephone: (518) 644-5941. Accommodations: three rooms, each with private bath; no telephones. Rates: moderate; includes do-it-yourself Continental breakfast. No cards. Children under 12 not accepted. No pets. Open all year.

Getting There: The house is three-tenths of a mile beyond the town of Bolton Landing driving north on State Road 9N; it's directly across from Veteran's Beach.

95

THE BALSAM HOUSE
Chestertown

The Balsam House just might be the *ne plus ultra* of country inns in the Empire State. It has everything: history, antique-filled comfortable rooms, superb cheffing, a superior site. The foundations go back to 1845; a half century later the distinctive Victorian belltower was added between the gables. Ninety years later, extensive renovation created a revitalized inn. It's sheer joy staying in one of the shiny clean, individually decorated, richly color-coordinated rooms; lunching on the front porch; Sunday brunching in the glass-enclosed atrium; or dining in the elegantly appointed main room, all candles, flowers, classical music, peach and blue napery.

Dinner is a leisurely affair with chef Ernest Doffe in charge of a menu that bristles with the brilliance of his experience as chief saucier at New York City's Four Seasons Restaurant. For starters he assembles interesting pâté's, vol-au-vent à La Reine, and he knows what to do with fresh mussels. His rack of lamb is a real prize winner but his duckling chambertin, braised sweetbreads and Adirondack trout are also admirable.

Located two hundred feet from the eastern shore of quiet little Friends Lake, on a slight prominence affording fine views of water and the surrounding pine-covered hills, this inn has something special for all seasons. Ski, skate, toboggan, sleigh ride, or ice fish, and come back to the Balsam for warming fires and a hot toddy. In warmer months there are water sports, fishing for bass and pike, and hunting for rabbit and Adirondack buck. Bring back your catch and Ernest will prepare it for dinner. For the golfer there are five 18-hole courses close by; the cyclist has more than 350 miles of paths, and the hiker a rich selection of trails. The inn also organizes sunset cocktail cruises on the lake. They are perfect preludes to Balsam House dinners followed by a retreat to the rooms upstairs, all wicker and cushy pillows, grandma spreads and sinks cleverly positioned in old oak chests.

THE BALSAM HOUSE, Potterbrook Road, Friends Lake, Chestertown, New York 12817. Telephone: (518) 494-2828. Accommodations: 18 rooms and one 2-story suite, all with private bath; no telephones; a television in the den. Full bar and meal service. Rates: moderate to expensive. Cards: CB, DC, MC, V. Pets not permitted. Open all year.

Getting There: Take the Warrensburg exit (No. 23) from Interstate 87 and follow State Road 9 four miles to State Road 28. Veer left and continue for exactly three miles to Potterbrook Road; turn right and go four miles until you see the inn on the left.

The Ice Augur Cometh
THE LODGE AT TROUT HOUSE VILLAGE
Hague

Hague proclaims itself to be Basstown U.S.A. (a title also claimed by nearby Bolton Landing), but it's also the town where the National Ice Augur Championships are held every winter in the third week of February. And until you marvel at those husky drillers whirling their arms so wildly, you won't believe how much ice can be penetrated so fast—some two feet of it in four to six seconds.

You can test your own muscular dexterity and then drop a line, or take off on skis or skates or snowmobile. You will return to a warm fire in your own log cabin; at this lodge the innkeeper keeps the stacks of firewood piled high. In the summer season he keeps a fleet of cycles, canoes, kayaks, and rowboats for his guests. Family groups usually choose the housekeeping cottages; in the main lodge building, favorite rooms are No. 7 and No. 8, with four-poster canopy beds and commanding views of the lake. They represent the latest decorating efforts of amiable innkeepers Lynn and Bob Patchett, who are always working to upgrade their property.

What started as a simple motel—demolished shortly after the Patch-etts bought it—is now an elaborate and immaculately maintained complex with four hundred feet of sandy beach, a quiet, almost sedate stretch when compared to the contrasting namesake tawdry town at the south end of the lake. There's a small dock, a nine-hole putting green, badminton and cro-quet courts on campus; golf and tennis are available at the nearby Ticonder-oga Country Club so beautifully tucked into the Lord Howe Valley.

THE LODGE AT TROUT HOUSE VILLAGE, Hague, New York 12836. Telephone: (518) 543-6088. Accommodations: nine lodge units and 13 housekeeping units with kitchens, all with private bath; no televisions or telephones. Rates: moderate. Cards: AE, CB, DC, MC, V. Inquire about pets. Open all year.

Getting There: The Lodge is ¼ mile north of the center of Hague, on State Road 9N, which winds along Lake George.

Steamboat Gothic for Family Fun
WOOD'S LODGE
Schroon Lake

For three-quarters of a century the Wood family has been greeting summer guests in their main lodge, in cabins, and in a four-story wood frame marvel of Steamboat Gothic design, built in 1883 and known as the Lake House.

The sprawling complex on the shores of Schroon Lake provides an ideal vacation hideaway for families who do not seek the fastidious or fash-ionable, and it offers plenty of lawn in a grove of towering maples where the kids can stretch their muscles. The beach with its rowboats and canoes is only a few feet away, and there's a tennis court and a string of Schroon Lake shops stocked with the necessaries a couple of blocks from the inn.

No meals are served, but there is complimentary coffee and tea in the mornings, and guests are allowed kitchen privileges in the main building. Here you will also find a television, a fireplace, an upright piano ("Alice Blue Gown" was the sheet music propped up when we made our last inspection), tables set up for jigsaw puzzles, an assortment of books and old magazines, and a general lived-in feeling.

The reception desk, presided over by Catherine Wood Querns, grand-daughter of the woman who opened the lodge as a boardinghouse, is a model of disorganization, but Mrs. Querns can guide you to such area attractions as Fort Ticonderoga a few miles west at the junction of Lake Champlain and Lake George.

The famous fort, captured from the British by Ethan Allen and his Green Mountain Boys in May 1775, is well worth a visit. Open from mid-May until mid-October, it has an interesting museum, beautifully restored barracks and blockhouses, and troopers garbed in Revolutionary War uniforms, firing vintage weapons and marching to the beat of the fort's fife and drum corps.

Close by on Moses Circle is Hancock House, and if you think you've seen it somewhere else, you have. It's a clone of the John Hancock home in Boston and now serves as an area museum and library.

WOOD'S LODGE, Schroon Lake, New York 12870. Telephone: (518) 532-7529. Accommodations: 12 double and triple rooms in main lodge and Lake House, four apartments with kitchens, and four 1-room cabins, each with private bath; no televisions or telephones. Rates: moderate. No cards. Pets not permitted. Open May 15 through October 15.

Getting There: The lodge is two blocks from the center of the village, on the lake.

Marvelous Mineral Mountain

GARNET HILL LODGE
North River

The name is an apt one. This mountaintop inn, two thousand feet in the clouds, was named for the nearby garnet mine and was originally built in 1936 to house the miners. Guests here can also try their luck at that mine—now abandoned—or wander on foot or skis along the twenty miles of groomed trails. Garnet Hill is a fully equipped ski center with instructors and rentals. In summer there's Thirteenth Lake down the mountain for swimming and boating.

The main floor of the rustic lodge, the kind of split-log structure that used to be found all over the Adirondacks, contains various games, pine trestle tables for dining, and a large garnet-stone fireplace, a magnet for the après-ski crowd.

The patio with its sensational view of the lake and the forest-wrapped slopes is a good place for summer sipping and supping. The food is not nearly as overwhelming as the panoramic views, but it's solid, and they do bake their own breads. The guest at the Garnet is not getting fancy fare or anything quaint, charming, or even spacious. He's getting the top of the mountain.

Fourteen of the guest rooms are in the main building, and they're functionally furnished, with bunk beds predominating. Those rooms facing the lake are the most desirable; others are in the manor house that belonged to the original mine owner. It was built in 1908 and is known as the Big Shanty. It has its own massive fireplace. Then there's the Ski Haus, with a large sitting room and sleeping loft, and something called the Birches, a four-room honeymoon hideaway opened in 1982 and blessed with grand views of the mountains.

GARNET HILL LODGE, North River, New York 12856. Telephone: (518) 251-2821. Accommodations: 26 rooms, 21 with private bath; no televisions or telephones. Full bar and meal service. Rates: moderate, with special winter plans including ski lessons and trips. No cards. Pets not permitted. Open all year except for two weeks from mid-June and two weeks from mid-November.

Getting There: 11½ miles on State Road 28 from the intersection with State Road 8 at Wevertown, turn onto Thirteenth Lake Road by a small store, the Towne Grocery. Follow the signs and the road, first on the newly paved segment, then to the old and then to gravel, all the way to the lodge, exactly 4.7 miles.

A Lakefront Budget Pleaser

THE INN AT SPECULATOR
Speculator

Speculator is in the Lake Pleasant–Piseco area of the Adirondacks, in Hamilton County, often called the Lake District of the Adirondacks. That means all kinds of waterborne activities, along with hunting in season and lots of skiing during winter months. Nearby Oak Mountain Ski Center is in the Snowbowl—with an average of ten feet of snow per season—and has a dozen groomed trails affording panoramic views of the mountains and lovely Lake Pleasant. There are also over two hundred miles of trails for sputtering snowmobilers.

Those mechanized marvels of modern man are usually found parked in profusion around this inn, their drivers resting in the simply furnished rooms or leaning into one of the hearty breakfasts or the solid dinners built around pork and lamb chops, chicken Cordon Bleu, veal Parmesan.

This inn provides clean accommodations at budget-stretching prices, and those tariffs apply in the summer as well. The inn makes a good base camp for partaking of some of the fun of small-town living: street dances in

Lake Pleasant, the flea market at the ballpark in Speculator, arts and crafts shows, a chicken barbecue bash at the Piseco Community Hall. Then there are all those lakes to explore and enjoy—Elm, Echo, Fall, Fawn, Hamilton, Oxbow, Pleasant, Piseco, Sacandaga, Spruce and Spy, T-Lake and Whittaker.

THE INN AT SPECULATOR, Route 8, Speculator, New York 12164. Telephone: (518) 548-3811. Accommodations: nine rooms, all with shared bath; no telephones; television in lounge. Rates: inexpensive, including breakfast; modified American plan available. Cards: MC, V. Pets not permitted. Open all year.

Getting There: From the junction of State Roads 8 and 30 continue on 8 a half mile to the center of town and the inn.

There's a Small—and Friendly—Hotel
ZEISER'S
Speculator

Gott sei Dank for the Zeisers, John and Genevieve, who have created what they proudly proclaim to be a "friendly little hotel" in the heart of the Adirondack Lake District. Recently refurbished and fussily maintained, it provides clean and unassuming rooms for those who don't like to empty their wallets when enjoying the wonders of the mountains. There are other reasons for finding this place. Namely, Zeiser Eis (ice cream) and Zeiser poppy seed dressing; they alone are worth the trip.

But there's more: good wurst for lunch, lamb chops, sirloin steaks, shrimp dijonnaise, veal Marsala for dinner, along with liberal portions of kraut, of course, "mit noodles." There's a good supply of beer and wine to set it all awash, but the highlight of the Zeiser bar is the collection of Scotch whisky bottles. It's a tribute to the mist of the moors and a dedicated collector's persistence.

ZEISER'S, Route 8, Speculator, New York 12164. Telephone: (518) 548-7021. Accommodations: five rooms, each with private bath; no televisions or telephones. Rates: inexpensive. Lunch, dinner, and full bar service. Cards: AE. Pets permitted. Open all year.

Getting There: Zeiser's is in the center of town.

HANSEN'S ADIRONDACK LODGE
Lake Pleasant

The rooms are named Norway, Denmark, Sweden, and Finland, each individually styled and color-coordinated, and as clean and modern as the countries themselves. There's a large "Velkommen" sign on the front door and a Norwegian flag waving in the breeze. Scandinavian souvenirs are for sale in the small gift shop, and, come Christmas, innkeeper Hans Hansen makes lutefisk, a foul-smelling codfish concoction you really have to be Swedish to understand.

But the bearded Hans is Norwegian. As quintessentially Norwegian as Peer Gynt. He certainly has a similar energy level, restoring a century-old house, building a picnic spot near a large fire pit with small bleachers for those who like to watch a Viking grilling fresh fish, tapping his eighty-plus maple trees to make his own syrup for dolloping over his special breakfast pancakes, working diligently with wife Marge to keep his own slice of the good life, Norwegian style, immaculate.

Breakfast at Hansen's means the freshest of eggs from their own chickens, home-baked bread, home fries, blueberry muffins, maybe even julekaker, Christmas cake, if you're lucky, and lots of smiles. "I like a house full of happy people; I want to give my guests mountain serenity and Scandinavian hospitality." Hans Christian Andersen couldn't have said it better.

HANSEN'S ADIRONDACK LODGE, South Shore Road (P.O. Box 28), Lake Pleasant, New York 12108. Telephone: (518) 548-3697. Accommodations: four rooms, each with shared bath; no televisions or telephones. Rates: inexpensive; includes full breakfast. No cards. Pets not permitted. Open all year.

Getting There: From the town of Speculator take State Road 8, turning right at the Camp of the Woods Conference Center; drive 4.3 miles on South Shore Road to Hansen's, which is on the left side.

Hansen's Adirondack Lodge

A Bluetiful Retreat

THE HEDGES ON BLUE MOUNTAIN LAKE
Blue Mountain Lake

Sunset-watching on beautiful Blue Mountain Lake is a restorative ritual, a romantic capstone of a day spent inhaling fresh mountain air, boating or swimming, or fishing the sparkling azure waters. There are numerous vantage points at this twelve-acre spread of rustic stone-log lodges and country cottages filled with locally crafted furniture and simple antiques. No accommodation is more than thirty meters from the water and reflections of the nightly red-pink glow show.

What better climax to a meal of home-brewed chicken soup, selections from a salad bar, and fresh ham with mashed potatoes and rutabaga, accompanied with oatmeal bread and followed by strawberry shortcake?

On chilly evenings guests gather before the crackling fireplaces to exchange tales of the day's activities. There's also a game room for the pint-sized set, a clay tennis court, and a spacious, book-filled library.

It's all part of a complex that traces its beginnings to the 1880s when a millionaire Civil War veteran laid the first stone. Later it was owned by the caretaker in charge of the nearby Vanderbilt estate, and today it's in the tender, loving hands of Catherine and Richard Van Yperen. They're a pair of innkeepers who believe in the extras—complimentary coffee and tea perking all day in the dining room, nighttime cocoa and pastries, a bounteous Saturday night buffet, picnic lunches for those activists who take to the trails or canoe to the many islands and shoals that dot the lake.

THE HEDGES ON BLUE MOUNTAIN LAKE, Blue Mountain Lake, New York 12812. Telephone: (518) 352-7325. Accommodations: 14 rooms in lodges, 14 in cottages, each with private bath; no televisions or telephones. Rates: moderate; modified American plan. No bar service. No cards. Pets not permitted. Open mid-June to mid-October.

Getting There: At the intersection of State Roads 28N and 30, take 28 west one mile to Hedges Road, which forks down a small hill to the inn.

A Cottage Colony
HEMLOCK HALL
Blue Mountain Lake

Another quiet hideaway that's a favorite with families of all ages and sizes, a turn-of-the-century ramble of mountain rusticity that's more informal and folksy than the Hedges, with a crowd of congenial vacationers, many of them repeaters. A middle-aged Syracuse couple encountered coming up the path from the lake proudly declared they had been making Hemlock Hall their summer home for seventeen years. They reserve their favorite accommodation before leaving each year—a waterfront, second-floor suite with a kitchenette and a splendid view of the fishing, the swimmers, and sailing beginners struggling with their Sunfish.

They seemed to know everybody in residence, those in the ten modest cottages forming a colony tucked into the woods, and those in a four-unit motel-type building; but then each night guests are seated at different dining tables—a sure way to meet and mingle with others enjoying Hemlock Hall. The solid fare features a single, but different, entrée each night, hard-to-argue-with selections such as baked ham and chicken, roast lamb and pork, and corned beef and cabbage, a particular favorite of those Hemlock alums who keep coming back year after year.

To burn off the calories consumed, innkeeper L. Robert Webb has trail maps for those who want to explore nearby Minnow and Sargeants ponds as well as Castle Rock. There are some sixty miles of trails in the immediate Blue Mountain area, including one that goes to the 3,800-foot summit of its highest peak.

HEMLOCK HALL, P.O. Box 114, Blue Mountain Lake, New York 12812. Telephone: (518) 352-7706. Accommodations: 24 rooms in main lodge; large and small cottages, some with kitchenettes, porches and fireplaces; 21 with private baths. No televisions or telephones. Rates: moderate; modified American plan. No bar service. No cards. Pets not permitted. Open May 15 to October 15.

Getting There: At the intersection of State Roads 28 and 30, continue on 30 six-tenths of a mile to the sign for the inn, which is a mile down Maple Lodge Road.

An Adirondack Great Camp
WENONAH LODGE
Tupper Lake

Jacques Cartier was the first European to cast eyes on the gigantic stretch of wilderness that we now know as the Adirondacks, but it took another three hundred years for the vast area to be surveyed. And that was thirty years after Lewis and Clark mapped the Northwest Territory. A half century later the Gilded Age arrived in the Adirondacks, in the persons of the Vanderbilts, the Rockefellers, and others of the super rich. They were there to carve out fiefdoms in the wilds, to build a series of structures to serve as mountain retreats for a period of months, weeks, or maybe only days, as escapes from the heat of the city in summer and as hunting headquarters in spring and fall.

These complexes were self-contained, with their own farms, greenhouses, icehouses, boathouses, independent water supplies, and, eventually, underground power lines—all serviced by staffs that outnumbered the owners and the string of guests.

They were the Great Camps of the Adirondacks. Similar to the "Cottages" of Newport, they were architectural fantasies, in some cases oddities. A Vanderbilt at Pine Tree Point in the Upper St. Regis Lake had his camp constructed in the manner of the traditional Irimoya form of Japanese temples. Marjorie Merriweather Post's Topridge, the last of the Great Camps, built in the 1920s, comprised sixty-five buildings, including a Russian dacha for her husband, an Ambassador to the USSR. Eighty-five servants were on duty at Topridge, which is now the property of the state and is open to the public for tours on the weekends.

Wenonah Lodge, built by New York financier Jules Bache in 1900, is also open to the public, for total immersion in the Great Camp era. There's a variety of accommodations in the ramble of rugged, though comfortable and expensive buildings, in the main house, the Bache house, and the Pershing house, built as a wedding gift for the son of Gen. Black Jack Pershing of World War I fame.

The dining room is a real treat: specially selected panels of birch bark cover the walls like an art gallery of primitive paintings, and there are giant stone fireplaces everywhere. And—an extravagance common to all Great Camp game rooms—a menagerie of mounted animal heads stare out dumbly at the skins of jungle beasts draped casually over hand-carved rails and wide-plank floors. The Bache/Wenonah Moosehead outside the lounge has what might be a record-breaking antler spread of five feet, three inches.

The lodge has been the property of Grace Palanza for the past three decades, and she's an outgoing hostess, who is happy welcoming families to all seventy-seven acres of this modern, affordable Great Camp.

WENONAH LODGE, Tupper Lake, New York 12946. Telephone: (518) 359-3265/9824. Accommodations: 20 rooms, 10 with private baths, 10 with shared baths; no televisions or telephones. Rates: moderate. No cards. Pets usually not permitted, but inquire. Open May 30 to September 10.

Getting There: The lodge is a mile from the junction of State Roads 3 and 30; there's a fairly large wooden sign leading to the drive.

The Woodsy World Is Your Oyster Rockefeller
THE POINT
Saranac Lake

Hidden deep in the pine-shrouded woods, on a prominence of rock overlooking a sparkling glacial lake, is The Point. It's far more complex than the name implies: canoes, boats, skis, a stuffed animal head here and there, an abundance of carefully constructed forest-camp buildings and furnishings, the kind one would expect to find at this retreat created for William Avery Rockefeller in the 1930s.

Owners Ted Carter and Jim Myhre are really better described as genial hosts entertaining friends at home than as innkeepers. Myhre is a chef of considerable talent, and the family Georgian silver and Meissen china is laid out for the nightly feasting on his triumphs. The following morning his fresh-baked wonders are delivered to each room.

Advance reservations are essential, for it's the only way to get through the security gate. Guests are greeted with a bottle of wine and fresh fruit. If the day is nippy, there's a fireplace crackling its own form of welcome, and of course there's nightly servicing of the rooms with a mint or something similar placed on the pillow.

Each of the rooms has something special to recommend it, and most of them have fireplaces. One has its own private terrace, a fine observation point for watching the many water sports, including ice-skating in winter on a lighted rink. For the nonwatchers, there are more than half a thousand miles of cross-country ski trails. In summer, boating activities abound, and come cocktail time there's a barge to board for sunset cruising.

The complex that Rockefeller christened Camp Wonundra is indeed a wonder, a nine-building assemblage of hewn pine and cedar shaded by towering conifers and reached by a narrow road winding through balsam and hemlock leading to the main lodge, the Long House, with its octet of reindeer heads. The ceiling is baronial, and there's a pair of eighteenth-century gargoyles standing guard along with a pair of massive stone fireplaces. In keeping with Adirondack Great Camp ambience, there are animal skins scattered about, and in keeping with the international background of host Carter, there are usually sprightly conversations at table.

In loyalty to his American ancestors, Carter, a lineal descendant of Governor Bradford, invites some Mohawk Indians to his Thanksgiving table each year, filling them with the kind of fare found at the first such festival at the Plymouth Colony.

THE POINT, Star Route, Saranac Lake, New York 12983. Telephone: (518) 891-5674. Accommodations: eight rooms, each with private bath; no televisions or telephones. Rates: expensive; American plan. Full bar service included. No cards. Children and pets not permitted. Open all year.

Getting There: Driving instructions will be sent on request.

ADIRONDACK LOJ
Lake Placid

If you arrive in the colder months of the year, the Loj, 2,178 feet into the Adirondack sky, advises you to make sure your car is winterized for nighttime temperatures down to −40°F. But at any time of the year, the visitor should definitely be acclimatized to life in the less luxurious lane.

It's a rustic high-mountain bunkbed hostel, usually filled with naturalists and enthusiastic escapists from their regular workaday lives who want to hike the trails and ski the slopes—especially those members of the Adirondack Mountain Club (ADK), which is responsible for the excellent guide to all the trails (with a most useful topographic map).

Each summer the ADK sponsors an ambitious series of three-day seminars along with Wednesday and Saturday evening programs at the Loj amphitheater, covering such subjects as local plant and bird life, wild mushrooms, acid rain, and proper hiking equipment, and moving as far afield as discussing nature centers in the Pacific Northwest as well as in Trinidad and Tobago.

If you really want to rough it, hike over to John Brooks Lodge, a wilderness complex 3½ miles—reached by foot only—off Route 73 in Keene Valley. There's a cabin open late June to early September, with family-style meals and a fireplace lounge for rallying around after a day in the invigorating mountain air. Two other buildings have cooking equipment. Grace Camp has six bunks and Winter Camp has eleven, and both are open all year.

ADIRONDACK LOJ, P.O. Box 867, Lake Placid, New York 12946. Telephone: (518) 523-3441. Accommodations: two large and four small bunkrooms and four double rooms, each with shared bath; three cabins with guests providing sleeping bags and cooking gear. Rates: inexpensive; modified American plan. Cards: MC, V. Pets not permitted. Open all year.

Getting There: Follow State Road 73 eight miles south of the center of Lake Placid (two miles east of the lakefront and the Olympic ski jumps) and turn at Adirondack Loj road, following it to the end.

Pleasant Placidity

MIRROR LAKE INN
Lake Placid

The pace at Lake Placid has slowed considerably since those hectic days during the 1980 Winter Olympics, but tourists still swarm there, especially during the annual competitions at the Olympic sites, the quadrennial selection of the American teams in everything from ski jumping and figure skating to bobsledding and the luge, and then the national championships each year on snow and ice. The Olympic Authority was established by the state in 1981, and it's in charge of the Ski Jump complex, in use year-round (plastic matting replaces the snow in summer), with a glass-enclosed elevator soaring twenty-six stories for grand panorama viewing; the Speed Skating Oval; the Mt. Van Hoevenberg Recreation Area (where biathlon, luge, bobsled, and cross-country skiing competitions take place); the Whiteface Mountain Ski Area; and the Olympic Center, the world's largest ice complex under one roof.

In summer, chairlifts run for mountain hikers, and there's a wealth of fishing and golfing possibilities, musical comedies in the Community Theatre, a mid-July Arts and Crafts Show, regattas, tennis tourneys, and horse shows. The second week in June brings the annual Northern New York Volunteer Fire Department races and parade—in its eighty-ninth go-around in 1985.

From mid-May until the end of October there are also boat rides on the lake, hour-long sixteen-mile cruises that will convince even the most scept-

110

ical that this is indeed an area of great natural beauty despite all the inroads of man.

The builders of the Mirror Lake Inn managed to retain some of that beauty on their eight-acre hillside site when they rambled their rooms, tennis courts, and pools on both sides of the drive along pretty little Mirror Lake. On the waterfront, the cottage with room No. 3 is a favorite because of location. A propitious porch overlooking town and lake along with a bit of lawn for lounging far surpasses the simple twin-bedded interior. In the main building the penthouse terrace rooms have cathedral ceilings, private balconies, individual decor; and in the building down the road there are less expensive, but certainly acceptable rooms furnished in Colonial style. Maybe management should have used a later period of time as inspiration, something to honor the memory of one of the town's martyrs, John Brown. In 1849 he purchased a farm at Lake Placid, ten years before he was executed for his raid at Harper's Ferry. His house and farm are now a state historic site. Brown and ten of his followers are buried there.

The inn has a pleasant staff, an outdoor deck for sipping and snacking, and one of the most attractive dining rooms in the Adirondacks, with wraparound wall-to-wall windows for absorbing the beauties of the landscape, part mountain, part lake, all lovely.

The breads, baked daily on the premises, are special at the inn; their produce is fresh, their dressings homemade, and they have a menu that just won't quit: close to thirty entrées, including London mixed grill, lobster Newberg, trout amadine, liver and onions, and such dessert delights as homemade fudge brownies, strawberry shortcake, raspberry pie, and a sundae slathered in pure maple syrup.

MIRROR LAKE INN, 35 Mirror Lake Drive, Lake Placid, New York 12946. Telephone: (518) 523-2544. Accommodations: 75 rooms, each with private bath, television, and telephone. Rates: moderate to expensive, with package rates available. Cards: AE, MC, V. Pets permitted but only with advance notice and security deposit. Open all year.

Getting There: The inn is on the main road that rings Mirror Lake, north of the Olympic Center in Lake Placid Village.

John Wayne and Claire Trevor Would Have Loved It

THE STAGECOACH INN
Lake Placid

Not far distant from the Olympic memories of the winter-fun capital of New York, there's a gabled two-story stone and wood echo of stagecoach days, an 1833 reminder that long before there were U.S. hockey teams, ski jumpers, and downhill racers, tourists came to these parts just to escape summer in the city. And they arrived by stage.

Built two miles from the village of Lake Placid, on the old post road which ran between Elizabethtown and Saranac Lake, the structure was originally part of an extensive farm and was known as the North Elba House. It eventually encompassed a small tavern, a stable, and simple rooms for post-road travelers, and it was soon established as a regular stagecoach stop.

It also served as post office, general store, and who knows what else, and in later years was owned in turn by the man who devised the Dewey Decimal System, and James R. Day, a curmudgeon of an innovator and a mighty force in the development of Syracuse University, as president and chancellor. In 1977 the present-day owners, the Peter Moreaus, took over, restoring the landmark while modernizing bathrooms and adding antiques and such fine touches as an old flintlock over the stone mantel in the common room.

Sitting in that room you can almost hear the rumble and the rattle of the stagecoaches as they gallop to a halt in front of the inn; and at night,

lying in an old brass bed, or lounging on that birch log balcony, you can ponder the past, grateful that this piece of an important part of Adirondack history survives.

THE STAGECOACH INN, Old Military Road, Lake Placid, New York 12946. Telephone: (518) 523-9474. Accommodations: five rooms, one with private bath. Rates: inexpensive, including Continental breakfast. No televisions or telephones. No cards. Pets not permitted. Open all year.

Getting There: The inn is two miles from Lake Placid via State Road 86 or 73 to the well-marked Old Military Road.

A Happy Headquarters for Cross-Country Skiers
THE BARK EATER
Keene

If you're curious about the name, check with a local Indian; it's their translation of the word *Adirondack*, a pejorative dismissal of tribes who could only exist in the shadow of the mighty Iroquois Confederation by eating bark. And if you're an enthusiastic hiker or skier you'll probably feel like an Indian traversing all the trails in these parts. But if you're only a beginner, have no fear. Innkeeper Joe-Pete Wilson, a member of the American Cross Country Ski Team in 1959 and of our Olympic squad the following year, is on hand to provide instruction. A native of Lake Placid, he's written a book on skiing, and has a ski shop with equipment available for rent.

Joe-Pete and his partner, Harley McDevitt, stoke up their guests with breakfasts of hot cereal or granola, homemade breads and muffins, eggs and bacon, lots of coffee and tea; and they'll pack up lunches and arrange for dinners—for a reasonable extra fee.

Then they stoke their fireplaces, one made of cobblestones and one of fieldstone, creating a cozy home away from home for those returning from the trails, or those who have braved the rapids while whitewater rafting on the Hudson River Gorge.

There's a warm, woodsy feeling to the common rooms and to the small, comfortable guest rooms furnished in country antiques and homespun. The names of the rooms are Bear, Chipmunk, Blue Jay, and the like, written on pieces of birch bark—favorites are the room with bunk beds and a small porch, and the cabin in the woods with a sleigh bed.

For those who want to hike for a week with a guide, or ski from inn to inn, there are special, all-meals-included package tours.

113

THE BARK EATER, Alstead Mill Road, Keene, New York 12942. Telephone: (518) 576-2221. Accommodations: Seven rooms with shared baths. Rates: inexpensive, including full breakfast. No cards. Pets permitted. Open all year.

Getting There: Take State Road 73 from Keene one mile west to Alstead Mill Road and drive north a half mile to the inn.

CENTRAL NEW YORK

Try the Tryon
TRYON INN
Cherry Valley

The name honors Lord William Tryon, the eighteenth-century Tory governor of New York—the Cherry Valley was then part of Tryon County, but that all changed with the American Revolution. The history is told in the Cherry Valley Museum, a delightful little display of and on Main Street America. A model of the town fort was assembled for the bicentennial of a massacre there in November, 1778; there are exhibits detailing house furnishings and equipment of the last century, clothing and accessories, hand-pump fire engines, the kind of melodeon that was manufactured in the valley in the 1800s, and a walking-tour map, essential for strolling the streets and discovering the history.

The museum occupies both floors of the 1832 Phelon-Sutliff House, a fifteen-room memory bank not far from the Tryon Inn. The inn is tucked into a grove of tall maples, carpeted with lush lawns. Guest rooms fill a separate building set back into the grove, away from the inn's fine restaurant, which serves lunch and dinner, with seafood and prime rib the specialties. Interesting antiques are scattered throughout the eating area, which has an outdoor patio for summer sipping.

Guest rooms, four downstairs and eight on the second floor, are neatly simple, with the general feeling of a lodge rather than a historic country inn. The 4½ acres of parklike surroundings add to that atmosphere.

TRYON INN, 124 Main Street, Cherry Valley, New York 13320. Telephone: (607) 264-9301. Accommodations: 12 rooms, some with private bath; no televisions or telephones. Rates: moderate. Cards: AE, MC, V.

Pets not permitted. Open May 1 through November 30; restaurant open year round.

Getting There: Cherry Valley is twelve miles north of Cooperstown; from U.S. 20 follow State Road 166 south 1.8 miles to the inn, clearly marked with signs on the left side of the road.

Good News for Cooper Fans
THE COOPER MOTOR INN
Cooperstown

The name honors this country's first famous novelist, James Fenimore Cooper, considered in his time to be "The American Scott." His father, William Cooper, was one of the wealthiest landowners of the new republic, and in 1786 he acquired some forty thousand acres around Otsego Lake and helped plan the town that took his name. The history is related in photos and exhibits in the Fenimore House, a solidly built mansion with a stunning Greek Revival portico and a treasure trove of Cooper family memorabilia.

There are more Cooper memories in the Cooper Motor Inn, a yellow-brick two-story Federal structure completed as a country estate about the time the author of *The Last of the Mohicans* was completing his *Leather-stocking Tales*. Owned and operated by the nearby Otesaga Hotel, this inn is fitted with an assortment of period reproductions, along with fine examples of the nineteenth-century real thing. The ambience is that of a private home, and there's the same pleasant sense of concern as is found at the landmark Otesaga, whose facilities are open to inn guests.

During the high summer season, late June through Labor Day, inn-goers are served a Continental breakfast on the premises; at other times, they are free to sign up for the bountiful breakfast buffet at the hotel, or to take any of their other meals there, and to enjoy to the fullest the many resort facilities.

For families or couples traveling together, there are two-room suites in the inn.

THE COOPER MOTOR INN, Chestnut Street, Cooperstown, New York 13326. Telephone: (607) 547-2567. Accommodations: 20 rooms, 10 with private bath; no televisions; telephones. Rates: moderate; includes Continental breakfast. Cards: AE, MC, V. Pets not permitted. Open late May through October.

Getting There: The inn is a block from the Otesaga Hotel.

Cooper Inn

From Stagecoaches to Shrimp Tempura
HICKORY GROVE INN
Cooperstown

For more than a century and a half, this hillside ramble of rusticity overlooking Otsego Lake a half dozen miles north of Cooperstown has been pleasing the public. Initially it was a welcome stop on the stagecoach trail leading from the Cherry Valley Turnpike, then a dining break for passengers on the steamboats churning the lake. Now it's a comfortable country kind of place where the soup and desserts are homemade and the pork chops are stuffed with dressing.

But the inn, built in the first decade of the nineteenth century by the Van Ben Schotens, on a land grant bought from the Indians in 1769, also serves superlative shrimp tempura, fresh fish, marvelous apple muffins, curried shrimp, and chicken teriyaki style. All this is done at the dictates of Polly Renckens, who with husband Jim has been keeping the inn loyal to its reputation.

Start a meal in this historic hostelry with a drink on the front porch overlooking the lake; or on a chillier evening, huddle around the fireplace. And when it's time to retire for the night, retreat to a room that's cozy country antique. It may be in Victorian style, or have a genuine feather bed. There's bound to be something blue around. Polly has an apparent love of that color even though the inn is painted white with red trim. But that's only the outside.

HICKORY GROVE INN, Route 80 at Six-Mile Point, R.D. 2 (P.O. Box 898), Cooperstown, New York 13326. Telephone: (607) 547-8100. Accommodations: four rooms, all with private baths, but not connected; a television but no telephones. Rates: inexpensive; includes Continental breakfast. Cards: AE, MC, V. Pets not permitted. Open mid-April through October.

Getting There: The inn is exactly five miles north of the Farmers' Museum and the Fenimore House.

THE INN AT BROOK WILLOW FARM
Cooperstown

Joan and Jack Grimes are responsible for this pastoral retreat east of Cooperstown on the road to Cherry Valley. Their 14-acre slice of serenity is about all that remains of the tiny, but once thriving hamlet of Lentsville, named for the itinerant preacher who rode the circuit on Sundays and managed a local mill during the week. Before the turn of the century there was a cheese factory in the town, along with cider- and gristmills, a blacksmith shop and a handful of homes. Today it's mostly this quiet little inn, nestled in the willows, shaded by the pines.

Just a skip over the creek that winds its way around the slowly rolling hills and through the overgrown meadows, the Victorian cottage of a farm house bids the cheeriest of greetings, beckoning guests into a fine collection of antiques that distinguish the two rooms in the cottage and the three rooms in the beautifully reborn barn.

Mornings, before you head out to the charm of Cooperstown, the Farmers' Museum, the Fenimore House, and all those baseballs, you'll be served a full-scale back-to-the-farm breakfast, featuring the freshest of eggs, homebaked muffins, a rich array of home-preserved jams.

THE INN AT BROOK WILLOW FARM, R.D. 2 (P.O. Box 514), Cooperstown, New York 13326. Telephone: (607) 547-9700. Accommodations: five rooms, three (in barn) with private bath; no televisions or telephones. Rates: inexpensive; includes full breakfast. Cards: MC, V. Pets not permitted; smoking not permitted in bedrooms. Open all year.

Getting There: Follow Main Street east across Susquehanna River to Estli Avenue, which turns into Middlefield Center Road (Route 33), to the sign for the inn.

Timeless Resort Elegance

OTESAGA HOTEL

Cooperstown

This grand dame of a water-hugging hotel has all the amenities, plus one of the most beautiful golf courses in the country, gently ringing Otsego Lake. In this age of plastic look-alike accommodations and ultra-modernity, the Otesaga captures an almost forgotten time, one of understated affluence and comfort.

Known to the nation primarily for its National Baseball Hall of Fame, Cooperstown is really much more. At the Fenimore House there's the largest permanent installation of the state Historical Association's collection of American folk art. Across the road is the Farmers' Museum, a fascinating encapsulation of rural life from Colonial times to the end of the nineteenth century. Rambling over a well-manicured spread of former farm land is a marvelously solid stone dairy barn, a one-room school, an old inn, a print shop, a blacksmith shop, a chapel, and other buildings brought to the site to provide a three-dimensional look into the past of central New York.

Also in town is the Glimmerglass Opera, with summer performances of such fare as *Rigoletto* and Gilbert and Sullivan's *Mikado*. Glimmerglass is the name the town's most famous son, James Fenimore Cooper, gave to the lake in one of his *Leatherstocking Tales*.

In 1838 Cooper wrote about his town that "the beauty of its situation, the lake, the purity of the air, and the other advantages seem destined to make it more peculiarly a place of resort," and the visitor today has no difficulty accepting the prediction. Today the lake is circled with stops the noted author made famous: Unca's Lodge, Leatherstocking Falls, Glimmerglen Cove, Deer Brook, Hurry Harry, Glimmerglass State Park, Blackbird Bay, Council Rock, and Natty Bumppo's Cave.

Start your morning at the Otesaga with a swim in the lake, then work through the groaning table of a breakfast buffet, following that with an invigorating round of golf before digging into the luncheon poolside cookout, saving the afternoon for a pilgrimage to Abner Doubleday Field, where baseball is believed to have begun back in 1839, and a walk through the Baseball Hall of Fame and Museum.

Appropriate dress is required in the Otesaga after six, in the Hawkeye Bar, the Glimmerglass Lounge, and the handsome dining room, dominated by a trio of grand chandeliers. The napery is crisp, the flatware gleaming, and there's a quartet that plays through dinner, then in the downstairs Templeton Lounge for dancing.

Meals are multicourse feed-ins, starting with such fare as chicken liver pâté and jellied consommé, proceeding through broiled salmon and roasts

120

accompanied with vegetables of the area and season, and concluded with fresh berries, pastries made on the premises, Brie and Camembert, all of it saluted with a California Cabernet.

The rooms are furnished with extra-comfortable beds, solid chests and tables, no-nonsense curtains and drapes, and the standards of maintenance are high; but then that's been the reputation of this classic country champion ever since its doors first opened behind those massive portico columns three-quarters of a century ago.

OTESAGA HOTEL, P.O. Box 311, Cooperstown, New York 13326. Telephone: (607) 547-9931. Accommodations: 135 rooms, each with private bath, television (on request) and telephone. Rates: expensive; modified American plan. Cards: AE, MC, V. Pets not permitted. Open from late May through October.

Getting There: Take Exit 30 of the New York State Thruway and follow State Road 28 south to Cooperstown; the inn is directly on the lake.

Strike Out for Dreamland
WORTHINGTON HOUSE
Cooperstown

In the heart of the Colonial charm of a village that shows great respect for the past, Ted Ott, a former professor of radiology at UCLA, and his wife decided to start new careers as innkeepers, sharing their love of this very special segment of Central New York with others.

They purchased this two-story Colonial home in 1982, 180 years after it was built. They immediately set to work: jacking up the foundation to make needed repairs, reworking the interior with its wide-plank floors, removing a giant hedge out front that was blocking the beautiful home from the public, filling the rooms with antiques.

Located a block from Otsego Lake, close to the source of the Susquehanna River and adjacent to beautiful Cooper Park, the Worthington House is next door to the National Baseball Hall of Fame and Museum. Opened in 1939, a century after the first game in Doubleday Field, the well-organized collection of some eight thousand artifacts and photographs is a bonanza for all those who worship at the shrine of our national sport.

The Worthington is a bonanza for non-smokers and those trying not to: smoking is not permitted. But then a tour of all the bronze plaques commemorating the base-running greats, and the review of all the World Series games since the first in 1903, is going to leave you breathless enough

to step next door, climb the stairs, fall into a comfy chintz-covered bed, and strike out for dreamland.

WORTHINGTON HOUSE, 13 Main Street, Cooperstown, New York 13326. Telephone: (607) 547-5281. Accommodations: two rooms with shared bath; television in parlor; no telephones. Rates: moderate; includes Continental breakfast. No cards. No children or pets; no smoking. Open all year.

Getting There: The inn is on the main street of Cooperstown, next door to the Baseball Hall of Fame and Museum.

A Stunning Tribute to Good Taste
HORNED DORSET INN
Leonardsville

Parents with progeny at nearby Colgate or Hamilton universities have an added reason to make a parents' visit: this incredible achievement in the middle of nowhere, at the crossroads of a non-town about forty-five minutes from the two colleges.

Antique-filled accommodations, handsomely decorated with considerable restraint and a proper sense of balance, ramble graciously through an Italianate villa constructed over a Federal foundation and frame, with a striking circular cherry staircase that's been in place since 1825. "Modern"

Victorian additions to the building date from the 1870s, the upgraded plumbing amenities from more recent years, during the time a small band of dedicated preservationists began their efforts to save this case study of adaptive restoration.

An adjacent building, a one-time community meeting house, was brilliantly revitalized as the setting for a special dining experience that begins in the second-floor library of a lounge reached by marble steps. On the ground floor, under a leaded-glass skylight, there's a formally appointed private dining room with handsome birch paneling. The main rooms are bathed in soft candlelight screened by hurricane globes and reflected in the Palladian windows, removed from a local school slated for destruction. A local church was once home for the gigantic iron kerosene chandelier, now gleaming atop a balustraded dais, near carved and stenciled black-walnut columns and cornices and an imposing travertine mantelpiece.

The kitchen and the devoted staff measure up to the challenge of this stunning setting, starting with the complimentary hot cheese dip delivered in a small crock.

Then comes the procession of freshness—salads with luscious redder-than-red tomatoes showered with chopped equally fresh basil, tiny spinach leaves freckled with feta and bits of bacon, cucumber slices soaked in a sweet, creamy dressing. During harvest time, the back room is blessed with local farmers' bounty such as golden ears of corn, the greenest of broccoli.

The côtelettes d'agneau chatelaine is a house specialty which translates to thick, carefully broiled lamb chops (what else in an inn named after a horned dorset?) with artichoke hearts. The roast duckling is partially boned and enhanced by a caper sauce that avoids all the cloying clichés usually encountered. Prime veal medallions are crowned with crescents of avocado and lightly touched with tarragon, then kissed with a sauce of duxelles, bedded down with perfectly prepared rice and lightly toasted pine nuts.

Sorbet trios of blackberry, peach, and kiwi are appropriate finishers before returning to one of the marvelous rooms, tucked ever so romantically into this historic home.

HORNED DORSET INN, Main Street/State Road 8, Leonardsville, New York 13364. Telephone: (315) 855-7898. Accommodations: two rooms and two suites, each with private bath; telephone in downstairs common sitting room. Rates: expensive; includes Continental breakfast. Young children not accepted. Pets permitted. No cards. Open all year.

Getting There: The inn is five miles south of the town of Bridgewater which is at the intersection of State Road 8 with U.S. 20.

College Cheer and Charm
COLGATE INN
Hamilton

On a village green in the Upper Chenango River Valley is this ultimate expression of college charm, Dutch Colonial style. Built in 1925 as an adjunct to one of the loveliest campuses in the country, this pristine white wood and stone tribute to taste—it looks as though it's painted every year—is a sparkling subsidiary of Colgate University, only a few seconds away.

After a swim in the university's pool, a round of golf on the excellent Robert Trent Jones course a half mile from the inn, or perhaps a dip in the lake or, in winter, a few runs down the slopes at Trainer Hill, check into the 1840 Tap Room. The brick and barn siding provides a warm, comfortable backdrop for the evening attitude readjustment hours, a welcome staging area for a meal in the inn's dining room, named Salmagundi. (The word means a *medley* or *potpourri*; initially it was the name of a dish of meat and herring, oil, vinegar, pepper, and onions—now it's also the name of the college's yearbook.)

Prime rib and Sunday brunches are among the specialties served in a room with candles, an inviting fireplace, and Windsor chairs. The well-kept dining room is matched by the guest rooms fanning out on the upper two floors. These have recently been refurbished and filled with the happy products of the reborn Hitchcock Company, with a wealth of stenciling on rockers and chests.

COLGATE INN, On-the-Green, Hamilton, New York 13346. Telephone: (315) 824-2300. Accommodations: 46 rooms and suites, each with private bath, color television, and telephone. Rates: moderate; includes Continental breakfast and morning newspaper. Cards: MC, V. Pets not permitted. Open all year.

Getting There: The inn faces the green in the center of Hamilton.

Colgate Inn

BRICK HOUSE INN
Eaton

Crowning a rolling slope of hillside in the fertile farm fields of central New York, this solidly built brick two-story is a tribute to a long-forgotten country architect who wanted to make his own Federal statement in the middle of nowhere. The bricks were baked from the clay at the nearby river and initially put into place during the 1790s, at the rear of the inn which was completed in 1807.

The views from the immaculately kept guest rooms bring to mind the song "On a Clear Day," and the 150 acres surrounding the inn offer all kinds of hiking and skiing trails.

The guest rooms are graced with antiques and liberal examples of the fine art of stenciling. The simply carved bannister leading up to those rooms could have been created by a Shaker artisan, but only an innkeeper with the friendly concern of a Norma Lamb could have assembled such a delightful assortment of artifacts to furnish her inn and to stock her little gift shop.

She also organizes afternoon tea in the best country British manner, serves dinners and lunches by appointment, and imparts a special feeling of friendliness, putting her guests and visitors instantly at ease, reflecting a love of the area and a respect for the past of this time-honored home.

BRICK HOUSE INN, Eaton Road, Eaton, New York 13334. Telephone: (315) 684-3655. Accommodations: three rooms sharing baths; no televisions or telephones. Rates: inexpensive, with special rates for skiing weekends. No cards. Pets not permitted. Open all year.

Getting There: From U.S. 20 in the town of Morrisville, turn south at the light onto Eaton Road and go three miles to the inn.

Home Is Where the Samboras Are
211 WHITE STREET
Waterville

Twenty minutes from Colgate and Hamilton, the pair of schools which bring such history and tradition to these parts, the little settlement of Waterville remains in a time warp of Victoriana. Flanking the town's Historic Triangle District are numerous examples of the elaborate house designs and decorations so admired in the last century. And not far distant is this three-story, crisply maintained home from the 1870s.

It's home to Carol and Stanley Sambora, community activists with a pair of college-student children—a daughter was responsible for the sketches and other artworks in the cozy little house, so bright and quilt-filled it could be called the Cheery Quilt.

On the ground floor there's a twin-bedded room with private bath, and upstairs, when the students are away at college, there's a pair of rooms sharing a bath, one with a double, the other with twin beds. All guests are treated to a full-scale breakfast with home-baked breads and thick jams, country-fresh eggs, good wake-'em-up coffee. And the Samboras will be happy to guide their guests to the attractions of the area: other Victorian homes, Cooperstown, Howe Caverns, and Old Forge (an hour's drive), and an antique row a few minutes away on U.S. 20. Then there are the "big-city" temptations of Utica to the northeast and Syracuse to the northwest.

211 WHITE STREET, 211 White Street, Waterville, New York 13480. Telephone: (315) 841-8295. Accommodations: three rooms, one with private bath; no televisions or telephones. Rates: inexpensive. No cards. Pets not permitted. Open all year.

Getting There: The inn and town are one mile north of U.S. 20 on State Road 12, which is also Main Street; at the Super Duper supermarket on Main Street, turn right on White Street.

127

A Home for Hamiltonians

THE CLINTON HOUSE
Clinton

This handsomely landscaped, carefully maintained inn used to be known as the Alexander Hamilton Inn, formerly a mansion built by a local lawyer, Othniel Williams, in 1826; but when the present owner rebuilt and restored it a decade ago he gave it the name of the venerable Clinton House, the town's most famous hostelry, born 1805, died 1920.

The accommodations are richly comfortable rather than elegant or antique-filled; and the colorful flowered wallpaper, matched to room accessories, is a pretty plus. The tile in the bathrooms is the kind that was popular in the 1940s. One room has a double bed; the others are single.

The dining room, a formal retreat with islands of napery, is popular with the locals and visiting parents checking on progeny at Hamilton College. The food is solid, the wine list select, and the service small-town friendly.

The ivy-coated college campus, spread along a slope in the Oriska Valley, is well worth a visit, especially the Admissions Building, once the home of Elihu Root, Hamilton College Class of 1864. A distinguished lawyer and statesman, he served as secretary of war for McKinley and as secretary of state for Teddy Roosevelt, and served a term as U.S. Senator. Along the way, he won the Nobel Peace Prize, in 1912.

In mid-July each year, the town celebrates Historic Clinton Week. Events are concentrated on the village green in front of the inn: a military muster, band concerts, folk singers, a pet show, and an antique car rally.

The Park Row street flanking the inn's side of the green was making its own contribution to the seven days of remembrance. There was a display in each and every store window on the block. Also participating was the building where two enterprising local gentlemen named Bristol and Myers started a company in 1887.

THE CLINTON HOUSE, 21 West Park Row, Clinton, New York 13323. Telephone: (315) 853-5555. Accommodations: four rooms, each with private bath and television; no telephones. Rates: moderate; includes Continental breakfast. Full bar service; lunch, dinner, and Sunday brunch. Cards: AE, DC, MC, V. Pets not permitted. Open all year except December 24 and 25.

Getting There: The inn is across from the Village Green in the center of the town, which is a half dozen miles from the New York State Thruway, from Exit 32 on State Road 233.

A Bonnie Not-So-Wee Hoose
BRAE LOCH INN
Cazenovia

At the western end of Albany Street where the road takes a sharp turn before passing Lorenzo, an 1807 mansion built by town founder John Lincklaen, there's a not so wee but ever so bonnie touch of Scotland.

The origins of the multigabled, brown-shingled Brae Loch go back to the beginning of the nineteenth century, but what greets the visitor today is pure Victorian, a grand old ramble of rooms, an instant transport to the Highlands.

Innkeeper H. Grey Barr is frequently garbed in a kilt; his waitresses in the six dining rooms wear them, along with tams, and you can outfit yourself in the inn's gift shop, the largest Scottish gift store in the state. It's run by daughter Sandra Barr Hughes, and of late she's added antiques to her inventory of imported wools and tartan plaids. Other family members are in the act, including wife Doris and son Tim, who's in charge of the sister operation in Jamesville, the Glen Loch Mill, a restaurant run by the Barrs for close to four decades.

Food is what built the reputation of the Barrs, and their two Lochs are famed miles around for fine fare, starting with complimentary hors d'oeuvres in the splendid cocktail lounge. They feature finnan haddie and steak and kidney pie, along with fillet of sole, which the menu explains is "not Scot, but hoot mon."

The downstairs pub of a lounge is a grand place for inhaling some of that mist of the moors, before or after indulging in the Loch's nightly dinners or their popular Sunday brunch—or before retiring upstairs to one of the antique-filled rooms. Favorites there are No. 1 with its double beds and No. 2 with a window seat providing a perfect post for those meditative moments looking out at the carefully tended grounds framing the lake. There are fireplaces in both rooms, but they are not operational. For the cheer of a hearth one returns to the dining rooms. A favorite there is the Grill Room, where the chef's on stage committing all that meat to the flames.

To quote Bobbie Burns, as the Brae Loch menu does:

> Some hae meat, and canna eat,
> And some wad eat that want it,
> But we hae meat, and we can eat,
> And sae the Lord be thanket!

Brae Loch Inn

BRAE LOCH INN, 5 Albany Street, Cazenovia, New York 13035. Telephone: (315) 655-3431. Accommodations: 12 rooms, each with private bath and television but no telephones. Rates: moderate to expensive; includes Continental breakfast. Cards: AE, CB, DC, MC, V. Pets not permitted. Open all year.

Getting There: The inn is two blocks from the center of town, across from the lake.

A Link with the Past

LINCKLAEN HOUSE
Cazenovia

The name honors the founder of the town, Col. John Lincklaen, who in turn was paying homage to Theophilius de Cazenove, a Philadelphia banker and backer of the Holland Land Company, when he christened the lakeside settlement. That was in 1793.

The Indians called the land *Owahgena,* "where the yellow perch swim," but land agent Lincklaen only saw fertile meadows and stands of timber, describing this part of the Cherry Valley as "superb" and "beautiful."

The solidly built three-story inn which bears his name greeted its first guests in the year 1835. Presidents and power brokers of city and state have been walking under its massive brass chandeliers ever since, heading for the lounge named for the seven stone steps leading to it, lunching on the outdoor patio bright with blooms, or dining in a formal Georgian room with white linens and Windsor chairs.

The guest rooms are comfortable and well maintained, and their furnishings and wall stencils commune cozily with the past. Number 220 with its extra sitting area qualifies as a suite; No. 216 is a snug retreat for a single.

The lobby reception desk is a marvelous jumble of just about everything, but in the stacks and racks you can seek out the flyers for self-guided walking and driving tours. Among the structures not to be missed are Lincklaen's 1807 mansion, Lorenzo, a gem of Federal architecture and now a state historic museum. Also notable is the 1806 Presbyterian Church, an 1846 library, an 1892 men's club, an 1847 Gothic cottage, and the Forman Store, dating from 1795. All those buildings are on Albany Street. Two blocks away is Cazenovia College, originally founded as a coeducational seminary in 1824. The buildings, including the 1853 Williams Hall and the 1857 Joy Hall, are mainly Georgian.

Among the annual special events in this town, which often seems to be the very definition of the word *sleepy*, are the Winter Festival the first weekend in February, the Arts and Crafts Show on the village green in early July, and a week-long antique car rally in August.

The Lincklaen kitchen produces solid fare for festival and show-goers or those who just want to walk past history. At night they sauté oysters in a dill sauce and coat large shrimp with Cheddar cheese before placing them on parsley-flecked rice. In addition to sweetbreads, bacon-wrapped chicken livers, escargots bourguignon, and scallops Delmonico, they have such all-American fare as leg of lamb, baked ham and roast turkey, filet mignon, and sirloin strip steak—all served with an endless parade of popovers.

And if that's not enough, next door to the inn is Wheatberry II, a food boutique with all kinds of imported temptations along with freshly made pastas, curried chicken salad, tabouli with feta in a pita pocket, Kahlúa chocolate chip cookies, and such refreshers as carob and "ginseng rush," apple, apricot, and blackberry drinks.

LINCKLAEN HOUSE, 79 Albany Street, Cazenovia, New York 13035. Telephone: (315) 655-3461. Accommodations: 25 rooms, all but two with private bath; televisions and telephones. Rates: moderate. Full meal and bar service. Cards: AE, MC, V. Pets permitted. Open all year.

Getting There: The inn is in the center of town, which is 18 miles east of Syracuse via U.S. 20.

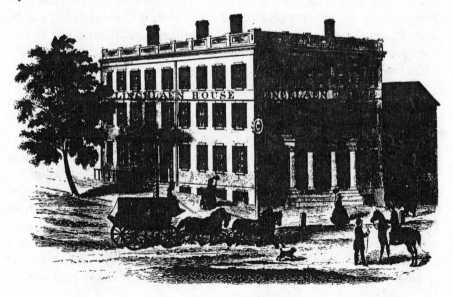

Simplicity Patterned in Stone
THE VILLAGE INN
Camden

Across the street from this simple little stone and red-brick two-story there's a cemetery with a plaque out front proudly proclaiming:

> Herein lies the sacred dust of our revolutionary heroes.
> Their noble ventures and lofty ideals
> Laid a foundation for the liberty of every man.

Also interred there is the builder of the inn in 1842, Gen. Lyman Curtiss, commander of the hometown boys, the Camden Greys. Later he served as president of the first bank in the town that straddles the banks of the Mad River and the west branch of Fish Creek.

The foundations of his home go back to 1796, the year Camden was first settled; and when he altered and added to the simple structure, the town was riding the crest of a prosperity that resulted from the completion of the nearby Erie Canal. Camden was called the queen village of central New York.

The history of the famous waterway is told in Erie Canal Village, eighteen miles southeast, where since 1973 a horse-drawn replica of an old canal packet boat, the *Independence*, has been gliding passengers backward into time.

You can take a twenty-minute, four-mile ride on a half-scale replica of an 1890 steam locomotive, visit a restored 1850 tavern, and tour a museum crammed with carriages. There are ole-timey stores, a blacksmith shop, even an old-fashioned church meeting house dating from 1839, one with regularly scheduled services during the season, which runs from early May through October.

In the village you'll learn all about the great engineering feat that commenced in 1817 and was completed 363 miles later in 1825. And if you want to complete the course, visit the Canal Museum on East Water Street in Syracuse. Among the memories is the last surviving example of the original seven canal weighlocks—the place where packet boats were weighed and the tolls assessed.

If you're worried about spending too much money in such pursuits, you should definitely check into the Village Inn. The rooms are simply furnished, the atmosphere rather spartan, but the rathskeller with its long bar and its pizza is a good place to relax after a day of sightseeing, and a useful locale for meeting some of the home folks.

THE VILLAGE INN, 24 Mexico Street, Camden, New York 13316. Telephone: (315) 245-2182. Accommodations: four rooms, each with private bath; television but no telephones; three rooms with single beds, one with three beds. Rates: inexpensive. No cards. Full bar service. Open all year.

Getting There: The inn is a block from the intersection of Mexico Street with Masonic Avenue.

A Boon for History Buffs
HULBERT HOUSE
Boonville

Let's make one thing perfectly clear: the Ritz it isn't, not even a Ramada or a Day's Inn. But history it has—in bunches. A three-story stone giant built in 1812 out of Black River limestone, hand-hewn maple timbers and highly polished cherry paneling, the inn has a grand two-level Greek temple–like portico. And through its massive columns the mighty have walked—just check those yellowed registers in the lobby. The names are all there, from U.S. Grant to FDR, from Horace Greeley to Thomas E. Dewey.

The history of the house and its town, named for Gerrit Boon of Holland, is told in a series of ground-floor murals, framed by etched limestone flanking the walls of the lounge, and one of the dining rooms is named for the Colonel, Charles Wheelock, who led the town's boys in blue south to battle the Confederates. Another boasts a curious ancient Dutch fireplace with an oversized chimney.

In those rooms innkeeper Mary Daskiewich keeps the locals well fed with what she calls "friendly fare"—baked ham with raisin sauce, roast pork and dressing, sauerbraten and noodles. She must serve it by the ton during the town's special celebrations, the Snow Festival in winter and the Woodsmen's Field Days in the summer, a salute to the forest industry. There are beard-growing contests, greased pole climbs, tree-chopping and log-rolling competitions, and the largest forestry parade in the northeastern U.S., one with bands and floats, wood nymphs, a queen and her court.

At other times of the year, there's a small-town calm and quiet about Boonville—and an abiding sense of history and place. In the square across from the inn there's a bandstand, a splendid 1890 Gothic castle of a house, and a fine three-story Victorian mansion now serving as a community center. Close by is a beautifully maintained white Victorian gem with red trim, posing as something from a *Hänsel and Gretel* stage set; across the street is a lovely large frame structure, the local Masonic Temple.

The guest rooms are functional and simply furnished. Again, hardly the Ritz, but what price history?

HULBERT HOUSE, 106 Main Street, Boonville, New York 13309. Telephone: (315) 942-4318. Accommodations: 14 rooms, eight with private bath; no televisions or telephones. Rates: inexpensive. Cards: MC, V. Full bar and meal service. Pets not permitted. Open all year.

Getting There: The inn is in the center of town, which is between Utica and Watertown on State Road 12.

Fisherman's Frolic
THOUSAND ISLANDS INN
Clayton

The Bass Anglers Sportsman's Society has proclaimed the 1000 Islands as having more bass per acre than any other body of water they have ever fished. Each year the 1000 Islands hosts the International Muskie Challenge Cup Tournament—during the muskie season which runs from the third Saturday of June until November 30. That's when the big ones are trolled—giants weighing in over 60 pounds, with an average scale marker of 15 to 25 pounds.

The Thousand Islands Inn, with its own private fishing boats (a 33-foot sport fisherman and a 31-foot open drift boat—largest on the St. Lawrence River), its special package tours and trips, its fishing gear and guides, has been home for the anglers in this area ever since 1897.

Whether hoping to top the world record muskie taken from the St. Lawrence at close to 70 pounds, or seeking out walleye, black bass, or panfish, the fisherman finds functional, highly reasonable accommodations at the inn. And a surprising array of good food with a menu that features North Atlantic sole, beef, Pacific chub salmon, sautéed frog legs, and a broiled brace of Carolina quail, and Long Island duckling—and sheer fun: brunch on one of the 1000 Islands, built around whatever you pull out of the deep, accompanied with eggs, bacon, French toast, pan-fried potatoes.

Every night there's something special: on Tuesday that means scampi in the garlic-butter-lemon manner; on Thursday chicken, biscuits, and mashed potatoes; and on Wednesday there's an Islander's Feast Buffet headlined by roast beef, ham, lamb, turkey. Every night there's a soup-salad-relish bar.

Dining room and lounge overlook the mighty St. Lawrence, which can also be seen from most of the guest rooms, totally refurbished in 1980. That's when the owners (since 1970), Susan and Allen Benas, recarpeted, installed paneling, painted, added to their inventory of private baths, and put in color television sets, retaining in the process a homey decor; after all, fishermen are not looking for the Waldorf.

But non-fishermen are also made welcome at the Thousand Islands Inn. They may simply want to enjoy the waterfront atmosphere, taking the Seaway Trail (State Road 12 E) to Cape Vincent west to town, following Broadway some three miles to Tibbetts Point and the Lighthouse.

Boat cruises, run from the middle of May through the middle of October. On board the *Narra Mattah*, a historic 1902 Elco fifty-foot glassed-in cruiser, you can glide over the waters for close to an hour, departing from the 1000 Islands Shipyard Museum with its interesting collection of wooden boats that span the craft from native Indian dugout and birchbark canoes to speedboats and displacement launches from early in this century.

Gray Line runs Seaway Cruises on diesel-powered double-deck boats every half hour. Among the 1,652 islands out there, the boats cruise past Knobby and Welcome islands, Swiss Chalet, Just Room Enough, Estralita Lodge where the first cottage was built in 1000 Islands, and Boldt Castle on Heart Island.

Boldt Castle was built by the hotel magnate George C. Boldt—the Waldorf-Astoria and the Bellevue-Stratford in Philadelphia were among his holdings—but it was never finished. When his wife, to whom he was intensely devoted, died suddenly, Boldt ordered all work stopped and some three hundred workmen, many of them European artisans, dropped their tools and went home, leaving a ghostly shell.

There's always something doing in this area, from the May Spring Fair and Craft Show, the Garden Show and rowing regattas, to the December Santa Claus Parade. This town, which celebrated its sesquicentennial in 1983, the old port on the Indian trail from the Mohawk Valley, the sought-over, fought-over city which survived three wars, has never been more bustling.

THOUSAND ISLANDS INN, 335 Riverside Drive, Clayton, 1000 Islands, New York 13624. Telephone: (315) 686-3030. Accommodations: 17 rooms, each with private bath and television; no telephones. Rates: inexpensive. Cards: AE, MC, V. Pets not permitted. Open from mid-May through mid-October.

Getting There: The inn is on the corner of Riverside Drive and Merrick, across from the Clayton municipal pier.

Thousand Islands Inn

You Ain't Whistling Dixie
DIXIE INN
Alexandria Bay

We don't understand the name this far north—at the crown of New York—but there is a quiet charm, perhaps Southern in its orientation, and the room rates are almost antebellum. But then the house is 125 years old.

Located near a flock of feederies that should satisfy most palates and pocketbooks, and not far from all the action on the Clayton and Alexandria Bay waterfront, this relaxed little inn, kept neat as the proverbial pin, is a reliable stopover for families who want to remain on the budget-stretching trail.

DIXIE INN, 2 Church Street, Alexandria Bay, New York 13607. Telephone: (315) 482-9697. Accommodations: eight rooms, each with private bath; no telephones; television in lounge. Rates: inexpensive. No cards. Inquire about pets. Open May through October.

Getting There: The inn is on the corner of Church and Fuller streets, across from the Alexandria Bay hospital.

138

FINGER LAKES
WESTERN
NEW YORK

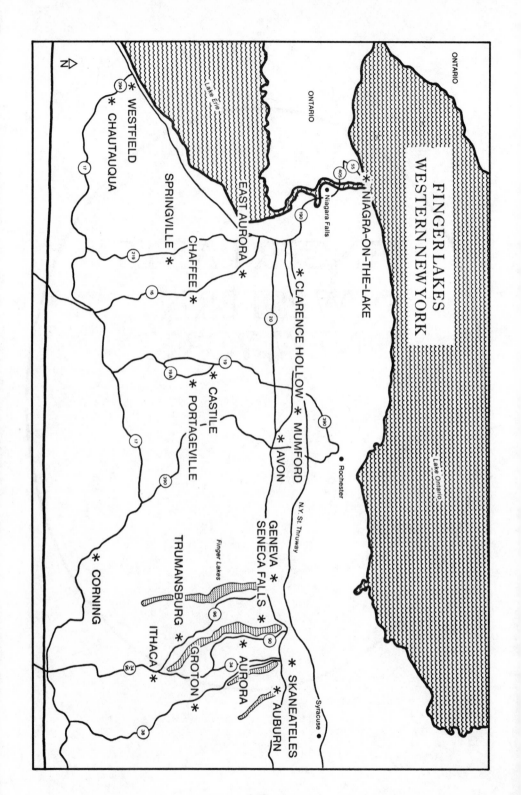

FINGER LAKES
WESTERN NEW YORK

ONTARIO

ONTARIO

Lake Erie

Lake Ontario

N

* WESTFIELD
* CHAUTAUQUA

SPRINGVILLE

EAST AURORA

* CHAFFEE *

* NIAGRA-ON-THE-LAKE

Niagara Falls

● Rochester

● Syracuse

* CLARENCE HOLLOW *

* MUMFORD
* AVON

* CASTILE
* PORTAGEVILLE

* CORNING

GENEVA
SENECA FALLS *

* TRUMANSBURG

* ITHACA *

Finger Lakes

* GROTON

* AURORA

* SKANEATELES

* AUBURN

N.Y. St. Thruway

140

FINGER LAKES

THE FINGER LAKES

Conesus and Canadice, Cayuga and Canandaigua, Keuka, Hemlock, Honeoye, Otisco and Owasco, Seneca and Skaneateles—not a Hawaiian war chant, but the Indian names for these fingers of water carved out by glaciers ages ago. The Finger Lakes are a fourteen-county chain of eleven narrow valleys spanning some ninety miles across West Central New York between Rochester and Syracuse. The glacial lakes run north and south, bordered by Lake Ontario and the Erie Canal on the north, the Chemung and Susquehanna rivers on the south.

There are more than a thousand waterfalls splashing down these gorges and glens. The highest, 215 feet, is at Taughannock, one of twenty state parks in the region. At Watkins Glen State Park you can walk under a waterfall and sit spellbound while being whisked forty-five million centuries into the past with lasers and special sound effects in "Timespell," a twice-nightly explanation of the birth and life of the famous glen. It's performed from the third week of May through the end of October.

Winters are cruel—with wind-chill factors, the mercury on the lakes can plummet to fifty below—but autumn is nothing short of sensational as nature changes its colors. Early October is best for leaf-watching, and it's also the time when the area's many wineries—close to forty of them—go through the rituals of the annual harvest.

Grapes have been growing on the lakes' gentle slopes for a century and a half, and there are regularly scheduled tours of many of the vineyards, followed by wine tastings. Taylor and Great Western at Hammondsport, founded in 1860 and 1880, a leading producer of premium champagnes and dessert wines in the country, has one of the most extensive visitor centers; they provide bus tours and tastings, a gift shop, picnic grounds, and free

141

open-air concerts during July and August. Several of their stone structures are listed in the National Register of Historic Places.

Glenora Wine Cellars in Dundee, nestled on the hills overlooking Seneca Lake, eight miles north of Watkins Glen, ends their tour in the Vista Room where the wine is sniffed and the visitor is overwhelmed by the panorama outside the windows.

At Gold Seal, on the shores of Keuka Lake, the tasting is conducted on a scenic outdoor terrace. The company, which bottled its first wine in 1865, has an interesting display of century-old documents in their handsome wood-paneled reception room, and at their dock the visitor can take the *Keuka Queen* for cruises on the lake from May through October.

Dotting other hillsides of Keuka are Chateau Esperanza Winery, near Bluff Point, and the Finger Lakes Wine Cellers in Branchport. At Naples, northwest of Keuka Lake, there's Widmer's Wine Cellars, and a tour of their facilities should be followed by a meal at nearby Wild Wind Farm, surrounded by explosions of bright blooms. Some of those flowers find their way to the kitchen—pumpkin soup is flecked with red nasturtium, leek with marigold petals—and the adjoining vegetable and herb garden has a lot to do with the freshness of what streams out of the back room.

North of Naples, in Canandaigua, at the northern tip of the finger lake of the same name, there's no winery for touring; but there are the incredible Sonnenberg Mansion and Gardens, an 1887 Gilded Age memory of magnificence, and an earlier building known as the Granger Homestead. The three-story Federal masterpiece, built by Gideon Granger, a member of both President Jefferson and Madison's cabinets, is filled with family furnishings and memorabilia, and in the neighboring Carriage Museum there are more than half a hundred horse-drawn vehicles.

Also in Canandaigua is the Finger Lakes Race Track, with 154 days of thoroughbred racing. It's the home of the July New York Derby and the September New York Breeders Futurity, which is run about the same time as the bicycle races around Cayuga and Canandaigua lakes.

The myriad other attractions in this highly appealing area are described in the individual inn listings.

CORNING

The city that glass built has much more than crystal to attract the tourist. On West Pulteney Street there's the Benjamin Patterson Inn, a beautifully restored reminder of what hostelries were like before the turn of the century—the eighteenth century. Close by is a log cabin dating from 1784 and a schoolhouse from 1878, and on the town's main street, Market, recently reborn, there's a grand variety of shopping and snacking temptations in the rehabilitated string of nineteenth-century buildings. The entire street is on the National Register of Historic Places.

One of the architectural highlights in that historic area is the Romanesque City Hall built in 1893 and now known as the Rockwell Museum. The name honors a principal benefactor of the restoration, the donor of a sensational collection of paintings, sketches, and sculptures depicting the great American West. Artists Charles Russell and Frederic Remington are the most familiar names represented, but there are numerous lesser-known painters and sculptors, including several from Europe.

The Rockwell is a must stop for another reason. It has a fascinating display detailing the history of Corning and its primacy as a center of glassmaking. Settled in 1835 by a group of Albany investors led by banker Erastus Corning, who bought two thousand acres (at $30.12 per acre) at the Erie Canal's new Chemung River link, the town quickly expanded, becoming the third largest shipping port in the state. But its glassmaking career did not begin until the Brooklyn Flint Glass Works moved to Corning, which was chosen for its port and the fact that inexpensive coal was available just across the border in Pennsylvania.

In 1903 an English glassmaker, Frederick Carder, arrived in town, and the museum's two thousand pieces of Carder Steuben glass tell his story in colorful, sometimes overwhelmingly beautiful detail. Especially stunning are the delicate sculpted surprises that were so difficult to make, the special Cire Perdue and Diatreta forms produced during the zenith of Carder's creative genius, from 1933 to 1963.

More of his masterworks are on display at the imposing, imaginatively designed Corning Glass Center, built in 1951 on the occasion of the centennial of Corning Glass Works.

The adjacent Corning Museum of Glass is a $7 million circle of glass, a time tunnel reaching back thirty-five hundred years, with seven galleries rushing off from the main room showing the evolution of glass use and manufacture through the ages. Some twenty thousand objects are on view, representing one of the largest collections in the world, ranging from a piece of ancient glass found in a two-thousand-year-old Roman tomb (shown here with a Please Touch sign) to an Amazonian Baccarat table more than five feet long—it was made for the 1878 World's Fair in Paris and bought by a maharajah who had Baccarat create for the top of it a three-foot-long glass boat, "a tour de force of glassmaking of any period," in the words of the museum director.

The same words could be used to describe the museum Steuben creations, those priceless pieces of perfection that are found in museums all over the world and which are colorless, absolutely free of any impediment. Consisting of 30 percent lead and made from an African sand found to be the purest in the world, Steuben is made with the kind of painstaking precision that only perfectionists are capable of. It's apparent when viewing the product, especially at the most complete collection at the shop in New York City at 56th Street and Fifth Avenue, or when watching the workmen at the Corning factory, an integral part of the Glass Center.

Etchers and engravers are on view, as is the "gaffer," the master glass-maker working the reheating furnace (the "glory hole") and the hand polishers. Steuben is the only major glass company in the world that does not add an acid polishing stage to its production process; final touches are done with pumice or jeweler's rouge, and any marks or flaws, any imperfection, means the piece is immediately relegated to the destroy bin.

There are no Steuben seconds for sale at the Center, but they do retail less expensive Corning products—Pyrex, Corelle, and the like—at close-out prices. Other glass stores, including the well-appointed Glass Menagerie, are in town, on Market Street.

In July and August, there's a nightly line of horse-drawn coaches on that street, rolling over to the Hilton Hotel, which has an interesting portrait collection of the movers and shakers of the town, everyone from Baron von Steuben (the Prussian General who drilled Washington's troops) to present-day leaders of the Corning Glass Works.

Summer is also the time when the Corning Summer Theatre operates, in another wing of the Glass Center, featuring top-flight Broadway hits. On Thursday evenings there are free concerts in downtown Corning, and on the second weekend in June the neighboring community of Painted Post celebrates Colonial Days with country cooking, arts and crafts exhibits, and a Saturday parade.

Color Quartet

THE CECCE HOUSE
Corning

Two blocks from revitalized Market Street, this turn-of-the-century gabled Victorian home offers an inexpensive, informal nesting-spot away from the bustle of shoppers and the teams of tourists oohing and aahing at the Glass Center. Innkeepers Margaret Cecce and Florence Gaiser keep a neat though cluttered establishment, filling walls and tables with a wealth of family memories, keeping a small third-floor common room for guests to make morning coffee and have a breakfast roll or some toast with jam. The rooms are color coded, named in harmony with the decor, and they're well maintained. The Cecce House gives the visitor to Corning the

chance to experience life in the slow lane, in the heart of a quiet residential neighborhood.

THE CECCE HOUSE, 166 Chemung Street, Corning, New York 14830. Telephone: (607) 962-5682. Accommodations: four rooms, three with twin beds, one with queen; all share a bath. Rates: inexpensive. No cards. Pets not permitted. Open all year.

Getting There: The inn is two blocks from Market Street, across Denison Parkway (State Road 17) and First Street.

So Near Yet So Far
LAUREL HILL GUEST HOUSE
Corning

A mile from Corning city limits, this Cape Cod cottage seems miles and miles away. Snuggled into the woods and surrounded by a picturebook garden, it's a country retreat at its coziest, with the most hospitable, helpful hosts, Marge and Dick Woodbury.

A few yards distant there's a spectacular view of the city and its Glass Works, its winding Chemung River, its rolling hills and valleys. On the lawn the Woodburys have furniture for lazy afternoon sitting or sunset sipping, and come the dawn, there are always the aromas of strong coffee, special teas, and fresh-baked muffins to tantalize the tourist.

For the quiet of the country, for the charm of an immaculately maintained cottage in the woods, for an escape from all the hustle of the large

145

hostelries found in and around Corning, Laurel Hill is a hideaway well worth finding.

LAUREL HILL GUEST HOUSE, 2670 Powderhouse Road, Corning, New York 14830. Telephone: (607) 936-3215. Accommodations: two rooms sharing a bath. Rates: inexpensive; includes Continental breakfast. No cards. Small well-behaved pets permitted. Open all year.

Getting There: From Market Street off State Road 17 take Walnut Street south, up the hill; just beyond the stop sign at Sixth Street the road becomes Powderhouse—follow it 1 mile to the inn.

A Rose Is a Rose Is an Inn

ROSEWOOD INN
Corning

There's more history within the walls of this 1860 three-story Tudor inn than most hostelries in the Finger Lakes can boast of, history that ranges from Herman Melville to Jenny Lind, from the Gilded Age entrepreneur who made a fortune from the Pullman car to the artist and illustrator who popularized the Gibson girl. The six antique-filled rooms in this amiable abode are each named for a famous somebody, including Frederick Carder, the genius whose mastery of glass led to the establishment of the Steuben Company, and Benjamin Patterson, Corning's first innkeeper in 1796.

Innkeepers Winnie and Dick Peer have assembled an interesting collection of memorabilia to fill each of their carefully maintained accommo-

dations: in the room named for Charles Dana Gibson there's an Eastlake bedroom suite; the double spool bed in the room honoring the famed Swedish soprano was built about the time she made her tour of North America; in the room named for the author of *Moby Dick* there are twin beds with hand-carved pineapples at the crown, some prints, and a model of a whaling ship.

Conveniently located near all that Corning has to offer, the Rosewood has another advantage. Morning means a selection of fresh fruit and home-baked muffins along with the coffee.

ROSEWOOD INN, 134 East First Street, Corning, New York 14830. Telephone: (607) 962-3253. Accommodations: six rooms, four with private bath; no televisions or telephones, but there is a television in a common room. Rates: moderate; includes Continental breakfast. No cards. Children welcome; pets permitted. Open all year.

Getting There: The inn is one block south of State Road 17, two blocks from Market Street.

A Rose is a Rose is a Rose
ROSE INN
Ithaca

Fifteen minutes north of Ithaca is this miracle on 34th route, a country inn of unusually handsome dimensions, surrounded by fascinating outbuildings on twenty acres of apple trees, towering Scotch pines, birches, spruces, and all kinds of maples.

The former Osmun estate includes this mansion famed for its circular staircase and heavy chestnut doors, and a swing-beam barn, a structure that, like the root barn, has recently been identified as a remarkably well-preserved building of great historical interest.

The staircase was assembled masterfully by an itinerant tinker, Will Houser, who suddenly appeared on the scene, was shown the stacks of mahogany above the hog shed (stacks which many craftsmen before him refused to take down to build an impossible staircase) and decided to stay. Two years later, he departed—just as mysteriously, but not until he had made architectural history. His staircase is a marvel, a timeless museum piece of highly polished, breathtaking carpentry.

His striking achievement is now the centerpiece of the inn of many rewards, happily under the professional pampering of the Rosemanns, Sherry and Charles, who scraped, painted, and hammered, and carefully coordinated their furnishings. In the process they created a four-guest-room inn of great class (plus two "overflow" rooms).

But then the Rosemanns are not exactly neophytes in the business. Berlin-born Charles is a graduate of the Heidelberg Hotel School, and in this country he's opened Hyatt Hotels in Richmond and Indianapolis, operated the fifteen-hundred-room Sheraton in Washington, D.C., and, before moving to his new endeavor, managed the Peabody in Memphis.

The innovative, indefatigable Rosemann revived the famous duck ceremony at the Peabody, that daily routine when the webbed-foot fowl are brought from their home in the hotel to parade on a red carpet to the lobby pond—to the beat of the "Stars and Stripes Forever."

Sherry was born in Texas, the daughter of a noted interior designer. She obviously inherited no little of her father's genius. But before she started decorating inns, she took a B.S. in microbiology at the University of Texas and a master's degree in social work. Somewhere along the way she found time to indulge her love of cooking.

Inn guests get some indication of this with the freshly baked morning croissants, the homemade preserves, the superb coffee—all of it served on china, crystal, and silver that expresses the Southern gentility of the blond Sherry.

She will also do a full-blown country breakfast on demand, as well as special dinner parties, exquisitely served. As one would expect in an inn with its own pens, stationery, preserves, nighttime mints on silver salvers, huge bath sheets, towels graced with lacy-satin trim, velour robes, and baskets of amenities including shampoo, shoe cloths, Vita-Gel, and of course Kölnisches Wasser.

The rooms are spring bright in color, with heavily flowered spreads and some matching quilted headboards. It's the very definition of a country inn, done with dedication and skill.

ROSE INN, 813 Auburn Road/State Road 34 (P.O. Box 6576), Ithaca, New York 14851. Telephone: (607) 533-4202. Accommodations: four rooms, each with private bath; telephone and television in common room. Rates: moderate to expensive; includes Continental breakfast. Dinner available with advance notice. Cards: AE. Inquire about children; no pets; no smoking. Open all year.

Getting There: From the New York Thruway Exit 40, drive 36.2 miles on State Road 34, to the inn on the left; from Ithaca follow 34 due north to the inn past the intersection with 34B, Buck, and Munson roads to the inn on the right.

Not So Far Above Cayuga's Waters

TAUGHANNOCK FARMS INN
Trumansburg

This inn's little flyer puts it perfectly: "Our foremost desire at Taughannock Farms is to leave in the minds of our guests a memory of pleasure, comfort and tranquility and the desire to return again and again."

The pleasure and comfort come from the close to absolutely immaculate state of the inn's housekeeping and the quality of the food offered in the quartet of dining rooms. Full-scale all-inclusive dinners start with a relish tray and orange-date bread—as good as the hot rolls, introduced by a Norwegian staffer years ago—then move into minted grapefruit, juices, apricot frappé, fruit cup dolloped with sherbet, or a soup of the day. That's followed by salad and one of the fifteen entrées accompanied with potatoes and a pair of vegetables. Among the choices in this ever-so-solid inn with a veteran staff is such all-American fare as roast turkey, duckling (served over excellent dressing with a non-cloying orange sauce and delivered crisp-skinned—as most diners like it), lamb, prime rib, steaks, breaded shrimp, baked ham, and whatever fish can be found locally.

The desserts, also an integral part of the dinner, just won't quit. Close to a couple of dozen delights, including angel food cake with ice cream and fudge sauce, pecan pie, peppermint ice cream pie in a chocolate crumb crust, strawberry shortcake, fresh fruit and sundaes, and a variety of pies that, like the breads and most everything else, are prepared out back daily.

Rooms are appointed in the Victorian manner in keeping with the vintage of the marvelous mansion, built in 1873 by John Jones, a Philadelphia

Taughannock Farms Inn

man of means who filled his home with heirlooms and imports from Europe. In 1945 his widow sold the property to the Agard family, who quickly established a reputation as innkeepers who knew how to please their public. Their grandchildren, Keith and Nancy Agard le Grand, are now in charge, providing exactly what they promise in an area replete with relaxing pursuits. For something more strenuous, a few miles to the northwest, in Lodi, you can pick your own cherries, pears, peaches, grapes, depending on the season, at Venture Vineyards, the world's largest shipper of quality Concord table grapes.

There's a hay-wagon tour of the grounds, a slide presentation explaining their cultivation programs, and a gift and wine shop to tour. But for wine buffs the tour of Lucas Vineyards in Interlaken, about halfway between the inn and Lodi, is recommended. Ruth and Bill Lucas harvested their first crop in 1977, three years later bottling under their own label and astonishing the competition by taking gold and silver medals in the state wine competition. That label, Tugboat Red and Tugboat White, was inspired by Bill's part-time occupation—or rather full-time half the time—tugboat pilot in New York Harbor.

Closer to hand is the Taughannock Park with its spectacular waterfalls and swimming, boating, hiking, and picnicking possibilities.

TAUGHANNOCK FARMS INN, State Road 89/Gorge Road, Taughannock Falls State Park, Trumansburg, New York 14886. Telephone: (607) 387-7711. Accommodations: five rooms, three with private bath, plus a two-bedroom guest house; no telephones or televisions. Rates: inexpensive. No cards. Pets not permitted. Open April 1 through Thanksgiving.

Getting There: 1.4 miles south from the center of Trumansburg there's a sign for the inn and park, which are a little over eight miles from Ithaca.

From Typewriters to Tournedos
BENN CONGER INN
Groton

Benn Conger was the first president of the Corona Corporation, and he built this mansion with its distinctive Greek Revival temple entryway in order to live in some style in the town where his company was manufacturing typewriters. But that's now ancient history, and a few years ago, when the successor company, SCM, discontinued their Groton operation, the town fell on hard times.

"But we'll make it; we're tough!" That's the way innkeeper Margaret Oaksford put it when we made our inspection of this transformed home. With husband Robert she works diligently at the task of making a success in the most trying of trades, running a restaurant. But she's ambitious, overseeing a menu with considerable imagination. Tournedos Richelieu in Groton? Why not, when the back room does the classic steak Diane, a baconwrapped filet mignon, and fresh chicken flamed in anisette, sprinkled with basil and scallions and finished with heavy cream, or flamed in Amaretto with almonds and oranges, or given a better than standard paprikás treatment, flaming a breast in sherry, then poaching it with sautéed mushrooms and scallions showered with Hungarian paprika.

With curried shrimp, baked ham flamed in Myers's Rum, a loin of pork flamed in Calvados and another with Irish Mist, the back room at this inn competes with the adjoining Benn's Den.

The inn's morning room is bright and cheerful for breakfast; the three other dining areas—the Cantwell and Blue dining rooms, along with the Conservatory with its walls of windows—are spacious staging areas for kitchen production. And upstairs there's a similar feeling of space—space rather than style. A favorite room there is the so-called Dutch Schultz suite. It's where the notorious gangster hid out for a couple of years while escaping the law. There's a wealth of walk-in closets for you to do your own hiding, an oversized bathroom, and a few antiques.

BENN CONGER INN, 206 West Cortland Street, Groton, New York 13073. Telephone: (607) 898-3282. Accommodations: 5½ rooms, three bathrooms (two private); no televisions or telephones. Rates: moderate; includes full breakfast. Cards: AE, MC, V. Children under 12 must be wellbehaved; pets not permitted. Open all year.

Getting There: Driving up State 38 from Ithaca and Dryden, look for the sign in the center of Groton on Main Street; turn left at Cortland Street by the Groton Hotel and go uphill a tenth of a mile to the inn on the right.

Came the Dawning
AURORA INN
Aurora

The year 1983 marked the 150th anniversary of this landmark hostelry on the eastern shores of Cayuga Lake. Forty years ago the solidly built structure was bequeathed to Wells College, which was established in Aurora as an institution of higher learning for women in 1868 by Henry Wells, the founder of the Wells Fargo and American Express companies.

It was one of the first women's colleges in the country, built across the lake from the Seneca Falls site where the first convention to discuss women's rights had been held twenty years earlier.

Since 1980 the site has been a National Historical Park, containing the Wesleyan Chapel meeting hall of the convention, and the homes of feminist pioneers Amelia Bloomer and Elizabeth Cady Stanton, instrumental in drawing up the 1848 Declaration of Sentiments, a manifesto on the rights of women. The National Women's Hall of Fame is also in Seneca Falls, as is an interesting little historical museum, a three-story Queen Anne mansion built to its present size in the 1880s on a fifty-year-old frame. There's a display of the history of the Women's Rights Convention, with memorabilia of its intrepid leaders.

There are other towns and villages to visit around Cayuga Lake, at forty-two miles the longest of the Finger Lakes, stretching all the way to Ithaca in the South. A flyer is available at the inn's front desk, which also has a walking tour guide of the historic sights and sites of Aurora, a town initially named Deawendote, the Village of Constant Dawn, by the Cayuga Indians. The ridge above the town seems to prolong the dawn.

Among the several structures deserving serious study are the remains of the first steam gristmill west of the Hudson, and Chimney Corner across the street, the oldest building in the state, erected by the Masons. Next door is the Leffingwell Home, with its outstanding Federal doorway and leaded oval windows. The Jedidiah Morgan House, dating from 1810, was the home of Lewis Henry Morgan, the father of modern anthropology. Glen Park was constructed in 1852 by Wells in a vibrant Italian villa style with bracketed cornices, a cupola with arched windows, and a sweeping circular staircase—it's now a dormitory.

Strolling the streets of this sleepy little gathering of nineteenth-century memories is a perfect prelude to dinner at the inn. Its menu is an ambitious one and changes periodically. Some typical appetizers include salmon mousse in a sauce verte, fresh asparagus with an orange-spiked dressing, curried shrimp baked in phyllo dough, and French-fried Brie. Entrees are

153

equally innovative. Some recent winners have been: duckling glazed with pears and raspberries; chicken roasted with lemon, then finished with vodka-braced sour cream and a hint of rosemary; loin of park stuffed with sausage and hazelnuts; sole enhanced with a tomato bechamel sauce; medallions of veal sautéed with flecks of ham and mushrooms, then finished with cognac and cream. For dessert what else but mocha-chip mud pie, a chocolate-chestnut concoction, or fresh-fruit shortcake?

After a dinner of such delights in a dignified dining room overlooking a setting sun on Lake Cayuga, you might be more than tempted to check into the inn, settling into one of the rooms, which in recent years have been completely refurbished and fitted with Stickley furniture.

A similar restoration has been undertaken on the ground-floor sitting rooms with their 1842 portraits of early innkeepers—painted by Charles Loring Elliott—and murals of early life in the women's college.

The pillared porch and the central hall with its gleaming brass chandeliers take the traveler immediately backward in time to a quieter, less hectic era. Nothing in the Aurora Inn experience breaks that spell.

AURORA INN, Main Street/State Road 90, Aurora, New York 13026. Telephone: (315) 364-8842. Accommodations: 16 rooms, 8 with private bath; no televisions or telephones. Rates: inexpensive; includes Continental breakfast. Full bar service. Pets permitted if arranged in advance. Cards: MC, V. Open April through Thanksgiving.

Getting There: The inn is on the main street of Aurora, next door to the post office and about a half dozen historical markers north of the main campus of Wells College.

Where Is That Again?
THE SHERWOOD INN
Skaneateles

Innkeeper William B. Eberhardt, who also manages the Aurora Inn, took over the helm of this historic hostelry a decade ago, succeeding a long line of predecessors going all the way back to the year 1807. That's when Isaac Sherwood, a giant of a man said to tip the scales at well over three hundred pounds, built a tavern to serve as a way station along his stagecoach route carrying passengers and goods from Auburn seven miles west and Syracuse nineteen miles northeast. Travelers bouncing their way from New York City to Niagara Falls found Skaneateles, about halfway between the two

points, an ideal stopping-off place, and learned to pronounce the place en route: Skinny-ata-less.

Eberhardt refurbished the rooms, filling them with antiques, and hired a kitchen crew that really cares and a front room staff that is always bustling about during the busy summer months when the dining room and the front porch are packed. On hot nights that porch is a must, for there's no air conditioning in the main room. But there's more than a touch of romance, sitting on the lengthy porch, looking out over the glistening lake, surrounded by glistening table appointments, white linens, tiny candles, flower vases, and hanging ferns.

Evening meals commence with the freshest of relish trays, some excellent date-nut bread, and such soups as freshly brewed mushroom. The lamb persille is a triumph, a select cut of the crown roast lightly sprinkled with garlic and shallots tangled with bread crumbs. The prime rib and the duckling, bathed in a plum-red currant sauce, are also in a prize-winning category. For finishers at this intelligently run inn, the pecan pie and pineapple cheese cake, both made out back, are easy to recommend with enthusiasm. And the wine list is not a greedy one.

Skaneateles, which celebrated its sesquicentennial in 1983, has two other eating experiences of note. Krebs, a local institution that has been in business since the turn of the century and which features a back-to-the farm, plate-and-bowl-passing pigout with all kinds of side dishes and fried chicken, ham, and beef; and the Old Stone Mill Restaurant. This was once the Tallcot Milling Company, and its present owners have done a fine job of adaptive restoration, filling the several levels with attractive tables under a mini-jungle of greenery and installing a menu that is one of the most extensive in the Finger Lakes. Prime rib is served only on Friday and Saturday nights, but steak Neptune is always available. It's a pair of filet mignon medallions sautéed in a sauce Espagnole, then crowned with a marvelous mélange of mushrooms, broccoli, and crabmeat coated in béarnaise.

Fairly fancy fare for a city that has managed to retain much of its small town charm. There's a mail boat that still makes a daily run from the town dock, cruising along the sixteen-mile-long glacial lake that locals claim is the purest of all the Finger Lakes.

Since 1969 there have been dinner cruises—between Memorial Day and Labor Day—three-hour shore-hugging outings, with prime rib at the center of five-course meals aboard the three-boat fleet; *Miss Clayton II*, *Pat II*, and the *Barbara S. Wiles*. There are also nightly moonlight cruises, weather permitting—and that's a perfect way to end a day in this tongue-tripper of a town.

THE SHERWOOD INN, 26 West Genesee Street, Skaneateles, New York 13152. Telephone: (315) 685-3405. Accommodations: 15 rooms with private baths; no televisions or telephones. Rates: moderate. Cards: AE, MC, V. Pets permitted but only with advance inquiry. Open all year.

Getting There: The inn is in the center of town and Genesee Street is U.S. 20.

Breakfast in a Basket
SPRINGSIDE INN
Auburn

Guests in this clapboard Victorian flanked by awning-shaded verandas receive their breakfast in a basket filled with muffins and sweet butter, fresh fruit, and coffee. The first guest to rouse himself from his immaculately maintained room with its floral prints and hard-to-leave bed has the privilege of plugging in the coffee pot.

The origins of the inn close to the shores of Lake Owasco go back to 1851 and a Dutch Reform pastor who opened a boys' school in his three-story home, thus hoping to help his pupils "avoid the evils necessarily attendant upon large and promiscuous assemblages of the young."

The pastor went on to greener pastures in Japan, and his home passed through several hands until in 1919 it was converted to a summer resort. Twenty years later it was turned into a year-round inn, and today it's in the capable hands of the second generation of the Dove family.

Bill is in charge of the kitchen which is known as the Surrey and features dark wooden beams criss-crossing a cathedral ceiling. There's a fireplace, flags and banners, an interesting array of antique lamps, and a cheerful staff garbed in vintage dress.

156

Special family dinners, enjoyed by throngs of happy diners, start with the house specialty of cheese soufflé and end with do-it-yourself ice cream sundaes or an abundant pastry dish. In between are generous portions of beef, chicken, Virginia ham, and a full panoply of fresh vegetables. The popular Sunday brunch is a guaranteed diet destroyer.

During July and August that good eating is followed by such musical fare as *Mame, Damn Yankees,* or *The Sound of Music.* The Doves claim they started the first dinner theatre in the northeastern United States.

Historians and students of architecture will find Auburn a kind of Mecca. In the nineteenth century it was the largest city in New York west of Albany, and many of the magnificent mansions from its age of glory still survive, especially along North and South streets, Market and Genesee. Federal troops en route to fight the British at Niagara in 1812 marched along Genesee, and twenty years later the Gothic fortress of St. Peter's Church was completed on that street.

Opposite the church is the Schweinfurth Memorial Art Museum, and close by is the Cayuga Museum of History and Art, begun in the Greek Revival style that swept this area in the 1830s, but completed in the Italianate style.

The Seymour Library on Genesee was designed in 1896 by the famous New York firm of Carrere and Hastings, and next door is an architectural hodgepodge of Queen Anne, Gothic, and Italianate.

At 33 South Street is one of the most imposing mansions in the state, a Federal masterpiece, home of William Henry Seward—governor, senator, and Lincoln's secretary of state—the visionary who purchased Alaska.

There are several golf courses in the area open to the public, and many opportunities to fish for trout, perch, pike, bass, and bullheads; but licenses are required as well as the rental of a boat, so check with Mr. Dove for precise information. And be sure to inquire about local driving tours

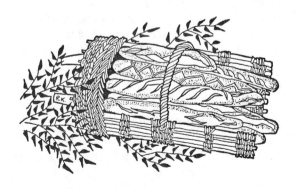

through the surrounding countryside, considered to be the most productive and historical farm land in the Northeast. At least that's what they say in Auburn.

SPRINGSIDE INN, 41 West Lake Road/State Road 38, Auburn, New York 13021. Telephone: (315) 252-7247. Accommodations: eight rooms, five with private bath; no televisions or telephones. Rates: moderate; includes Continental breakfast. Full bar service. Pets not permitted. Cards: MC, V. Open February through December.

Getting There: The inn is a mile from the center of town, four-tenths of a mile from the traffic circle on Lake Owasco on State Road 38 South, which twists through the town and the residential area.

Downtown Is Inn
THE GOULD
Seneca Falls

Seneca Falls' proudest piece of downtown of 150 years ago served travelers of stage, train, and boat until the Great Fire of 1890 claimed it and eighty-five other buildings in town. But the town rallied and rebuilt. Alas, in 1918 another blaze huffed and puffed and burned the house down. But then came Norman Gould of Gould Pumps; he envisioned the hotel as "a necessity for the town's continuance and prosperity." And he made sure it would not burn again—portland cement and Bessemer Process steel were used to rebuild.

The inn officially reopened in February 1920 still stands today, bearing the name of its savior and final founder. There are seven suites, each of them decorated individually with a scattering of antiques from various periods of the inn's history. Two suites are called "executive bedrooms"; another two have a kitchen along with a small living room, and three others have a more spacious living room along with a kitchen, bedroom, and bath.

In 1981 there was a restoration of these and other rooms, including the dining room named for Elizabeth Cady Stanton, who, with Lucretia Mott and other famous feminists, was responsible for the first Women's Rights Convention, held in Seneca Falls in 1848.

The Pump Room honors the Gould Industry, which makes pumps and is the major manufacturer in the area. Sunday brunch is the outstanding meal at the Gould. The rest of the food is fairly standard—beef, seafood, poultry with some mild attempts at French and Italian saucing—and for the bargain-mavens there are early dinners served before 7:00 at budget-pleasing prices.

The Gould

THE GOULD, 108 Fall Street, Seneca Falls, New York 13148. Telephone: (315) 568-5801. Accommodations: seven suites, each with private bath, television, and telephones. Rates: moderate. Lunch, dinner, Sunday brunch, and full bar service. Cards: AC, CB, DC, MC, V. Open all year.

Getting There: The inn is in the center of town on routes 5 and 20.

A Renaissance Retreat
GENEVA ON THE LAKE
Geneva

This stunning structure, with its ten acres of formal gardens and its super-sized pool guarded by classical statuary, pillars, and terra-cotta urns, is easily one of the finest, most impressive inns in this—or any other—book of memorable overnighting experiences.

The three-story stucco mansion with its red tile roof is an Italian villa of the monstrous size—large enough to qualify as a *palazzo*. When it was built in 1911 by the widow of the founder of the prosperous Geneva Malt House, it was modeled after a sixteenth-century villa in Frascati, near Rome.

Minnie Matthews Nestor could as easily have been inspired by Italian structures much closer to home: Sonnenberg Gardens in Canandaigua, seventeen miles west of Geneva. There the founder of the First National City Bank had a mansion, and his widow planned and organized an Italian garden, complete with sunken parterres and a Neptune fountain. Mary Clark Thompson also had extensive rose and pansy gardens, a Roman bath, and a temple of Diana. Her achievement, carefully restored and opened to the public in 1973, was termed by the Smithsonian "one of the most magnificent late-Victorian gardens ever created in America."

Other homes and gardens to visit in this jewel of a town on Seneca Lake include the Prouty-Chew House, an 1825 Federal masterpiece on Main Street that doubles as a headquarters and museum of the Geneva Historical Society, and Rose Hill, an elegant 1839 expression of Greek Revival located east of town.

Geneva is also the home of Hobart and William Smith colleges, founded respectively in 1822 and 1908. It's often referred to as the City of Churches, and each year during Memorial Day weekend, it's the City of Trout, with a very popular Lake Trout Derby. Winter brings ice skating in the extensive city recreation center, and the autumn an invasion of apple pickers and buyers.

New York is the second-largest apple-producing state in the nation, and the Mcintosh is king—some 319 million pounds are produced a year. Red Jacket Orchards a mile west of Geneva is an apple lover's dream, with 225 acres of fruit trees—a total of fifty thousand—many of them dating from 1917. Thanks to modern cold storage methods, much of that fruit is available year round, as is the superb Red Jacket cider.

Guests at this stunning Renaissance retreat can bring the jugs back to their super-luxe suites, each of which has a living room, one or two bedrooms, a full bath or bath and a half, and a kitchen. Some have a private balcony or fireplace, and almost all face the lake, where the morning sunrise is a sight not to be missed.

A bottle of New York State wine greets arriving guests, along with flowers and a fruit basket. Continental breakfasts are complimentary, and on Friday nights there's a wine and cheese party on the terrace. On Sundays there's a grand buffet of a dinner—all included in the rates.

Since November 1981, when new owners took over from the Capuchin Order who ran the mansion as a monastery from 1949 until 1973, there have been suites open to the public. Initially there were only three; now there are twenty-nine. Each of them is a superior accommodation, individually decorated and very carefully color coordinated, including all the linens.

GENEVA ON THE LAKE, 1001 Lohkland Road/State Route 14S, Geneva, New York 14456. Telephone: (315) 789-7190. Accommodations: 29 suites, each with private bath, kitchen, television, clock-radio, telephone. Rates: very expensive; includes Continental breakfast, Friday wine and cheese, Sunday buffet. Cards: AE, MC, V. Pets not permitted. Open all year.

Getting There: The inn is a mile south from the junction of U.S. Routes 5 and 20 on Route 14 South.

Richardson Romanesque in the Finger Lakes

THE INN AT BELHURST CASTLE
Geneva

The year 1985 marks the centennial of this red Medina-stone fortress named for the beautiful forest that surrounds it—at least in part. Other mansions have been built along the western shores of Lake Seneca, but there are still towering, stately oak trees on these well-manicured twenty-five acres of bluff with a commanding view of the water.

Woodcarvers were imported from Europe to work the mahogany and oak of the castle; much of the material was imported also. The cost of construction was a staggering $475,000, and there's considerable lore and legend about this museum of a mansion. With more stained glass than most churches can claim, it is filled with paintings and statuary. A wooden bust of the architect has been placed in a special niche in the massive carved staircase.

A total of eight fireplaces are wedged into the walls, each of them sporting a distinctive tile or wood frame, and on one of the landings a spigot originally installed to dispense ice water now pours white wine, presumably from one of the Finger Lakes wineries. A bedroom, unconventionally half-Oriental in design, overwhelms the guest with stained glass; another, the Dwyer suite, features an antique mahogany giant of a four-poster bed with equally massive mahogany chairs. The name honors Cornelius "Red" Dwyer, a notable if not notorious sportsman and gambler who converted the castle into a restaurant and casino. He remained in command until his death at age ninety-three.

The present owners restored this Romanesque retreat built in the grand Richardson manner. On Sundays there's brunch and during the season a noontime buffet in this, one of the grandest of the Gilded Age mansions built in the late medieval manner.

THE INN AT BELHURST CASTLE, Lockland Road/State Road 14
(P.O. Box 609), Geneva, New York 14456. Telephone: (315) 781-0201.
Accommodations: nine rooms and three suites, each with private bath; no
televisions or telephones. Rates: expensive. Cards: AE, MC, V. Pets not
permitted. Open all year.

Getting There: The inn is at the southern end of the city limits, 1.5 miles
from the junction of Route 13 with 20 and 5.

Avon Calling!

AVON INN
Avon

This handsomely pillared white giant of a Greek Revival masterpiece was
built in 1820 for wealthy farmer Jonathan H. Gerry—broom corn was his
specialty. After the Civil War it was converted to a health center, and then to
a sanitarium noted for its nearby waters. The strong-smelling liquid from
the sulphur springs was regarded as a cure for all kinds of maladies: malaria
and rheumatism, various diseases of the liver and kidneys. Southern aris-
tocrats somehow found their way to this antebellum beauty in the Genesee
Valley, along with the likes of Ford and Edison, George Eastman, and, of
course, the ubiquitous Eleanor Roosevelt.

The Avon Inn boasted the first elevator in upstate New York, it had the
first central heating system in the valley and the first bank and post office,
and it was a stop on the Underground Railroad.

And since November 1982, when the present innkeepers took over, it's
been something to recommend on the country inn trail. Badly damaged by
fire in 1979 but carefully restored, it's now a special step into the past, with
pleasantly appointed rooms (a favorite is No. 120, the bridal room with its
own Jacuzzi) and dining rooms that seat twenty-five to two hundred.

For lunch there are crêpes, quiches, and omelets of the day, along with
excellent copper kettle bisque, potato skins fried with bacon and Cheddar,
and good sandwiches. Dinner spells chicken Cordon Bleu and beef Wellington, along with roast duck, lamb chops, roast pork loin, New York strip
steak, and a variety of seafood, veal, and chicken dishes. Desserts include
hot apple pie and fresh strawberry pie. And many come calling for Sunday's
buffet brunch.

AVON INN, 55 East Main Street (U.S. 20 and State Road 5), Avon, New York 14414. Telephone: (716) 226-8181. Accommodations: 16 rooms, each with private bath, most with television; no telephones. Rates: inexpensive; package rates available with dinner included in rate. Cards: AE, MC, V. Children welcome. Open all year.

Getting There: The inn is on the corner of East Main Street and Temple Street, near the traffic circle in the center of Avon.

Stenciling Supreme

GENESEE COUNTRY INN
Mumford

On the 150th anniversary of this solid stone structure, positioned where Allen and Spring creeks pour their waters into the Oatka, Glenda and Greg Barcklow opened it as an inn. They started with just five rooms, and then, with the same tasteful direction and the talents of several local artists, added another five.

Each of the rooms is individually designed, hand stenciled by Ruth Flowers and Kat McCormick, a dynamic duo of Rochester master craftspeople who specialize in that art, along with theorems and fireboards. Thus in the MacNaughton Room (each of the rooms is named after a prominent resident of the area), a double with splendid views of the surrounding woods and Allen Creek, there's a daisy chain stenciled on the walls, along with green, gold, and orange leaves. In the McQueen, the stenciling is red, to

164

match the calico curtains; in the DeFazio the theme of hearts is carried out with stencils of pale blue and beige, and the curtains are natural-colored and ruffled, Colonial style.

Stenciling is also found in the small kitchen, where the Continental breakfasts of orange juice, fresh croissants, and such treats as blueberry muffins are prepared, and in the sitting room, the library with its television set and a splendid folk art mural by Flowers, and marching up the stairs.

Each of the guest rooms is a special experience, and the Barcklows have taken the fine art of innkeeping to new levels by providing a gaily tied package of amenities: hair spray, a razor, aloe skin cream, toothpaste, shampoo, and conditioner. Flowers and plants are also used liberally, there's a special greeting card on the bed for each new guest and a newspaper in the morning, and newlyweds—this is a grand place for them—are given a bottle of champagne on arrival.

The six acres of creeks, waterfalls, woods, ponds, and ducks, along with the porch and terraces, are great escapes from the bustle of the big city, yet Buffalo is one hour away and Rochester only thirty minutes. Again and again one is reminded of the definition of the Iroquois word, *genesee*— "pleasant valley."

The inn, which opened in 1983, is only eight-tenths of a mile from the Genesee Country Village and Museum, 125 acres depicting life in the nineteenth century. Among the half a hundred buildings on the grounds is a curious octagon home built in the 1870s, a sparkling white Greek Revival mansion from the 1830s, a museum of more than forty carriages, and a fine gallery devoted to the sporting life—paintings, prints, and bronze sculptures showing game animals and hunting and fishing scenes. Open from the second weekend in May through the third weekend in October, the village is the scene of many special events, including a mid-May Highland gathering of four Scottish bands and more than a hundred bagpipers, a mid-June festival of string bands from all over the East playing nineteenth-century music, and dressage demonstrations and competitions. July Fourth is celebrated with a vengeance, and in mid-July there's the annual re-creation of the Battle of Gettysburg. The first week in October brings a nineteenth-century agricultural fair.

GENESEE COUNTRY INN, 948 George Street, Mumford, New York 14511. Telephone: (716) 538-2500. Accommodations: ten rooms, each with private bath; clock-radios; television in library; some telephones. Rates: moderate; includes Continental breakfast. Cards: AE, MC, V. No children under 12; pets not permitted. Open all year.

Getting There: Mumford is 16 miles from metropolitan Rochester, located off New York Thruway exits 46 and 47 and the Avon Exit of I-390.

Live in a Park
GLEN IRIS INN
Castile

Thirty-five miles south of Rochester is a world apart: a world of mighty waterfalls and gorgeous gorges, shales and sandstones, canyons and valleys, lush forest and winding river, a world of 14,350 acres known as the Letchworth State Park.

Named for William Pryor Letchworth, a nineteenth-century entrepreneur and philanthropist, one-time president of the Buffalo Fine Arts Academy, and amateur historian fascinated by the Indians, the park includes a thousand acres, three waterfalls, and land on both sides of the Genesee River deeded by Letchworth to the state on his death in 1910.

In the heart of his wilderness estate was the home he purchased in 1859 and christened Glen Iris. Operated for a time as a temperance tavern, the three-story mansion with its wonderful wraparound pillared porch started its Genesee Valley life as a simple frame home in the 1820s.

Today it's the happy province of Peter, Cora, and Paula Pizzutelli, who operate the bustling inn and its excellent restaurant, one with a menu that runs the gamut from escargots bourguignon and Chinese egg rolls to fully garnished nova, from sautéed rainbow trout amadine to lamb shanks jardinière. The veal is plume de veau from Wisconsin, the king crab legs are from Alaska, the array of freshness at the relish and salad table is from the local land. With twenty-four hours' notice, the back room will prepare anything desired. A regular item on the menu is the breast of chicken Chesapeake, a creation of the American Culinary Team that won a gold medal for it in the 1980 Culinary Olympics: the breast is filled with ham and crab, fresh mushrooms and scallions, seasoned with something special, and topped with a brandy-spiked cream sauce, then served over a nest of sautéed spinach and cheese-buttered fettuccine.

It's the stuff dreams are made on, especially if you retire to one of the inn rooms after indulging in such innovative artistry. Each of the guest rooms is named after a different tree found in the park. Birch and Cherry have a view of the falls and are rather spacious; Linden is the smallest and can be considered an overflow room, but it's cozy.

The dark oak and chestnut paneling and railing on the staircase is a work of art, and those Swiss cowbells hanging here and there are testimony to the fact that William Letchworth, ever the innovator, imported Swiss cows to improve local herds. The nineteenth-century pictures on the walls leading up to the rooms lend an added air of authenticity to those simple, but relaxed and woodsy quarters, which serve as a comfortable bivouac for exploring natural phenomena just outside the inn door. Pick up a trail map

166

Glen Iris Inn

at the front desk, and make sure the restored Seneca Indian Council House and the nearby Museum of Pioneer and Indian History are on your itinerary as you wander around the park. They're both there because of Letchworth.

GLEN IRIS INN, Letchworth State Park, Castile, New York 14427. Telephone: (716) 493-2622. Accommodations: 21 rooms, each with private bath; no televisions or telephones, but a third-floor sitting room overlooking the falls does have a television. Rates: inexpensive to moderate. Full meal and bar service. Cards: AE, MC, V. Pets not permitted. Open from Easter through October.

Getting There: The park can be entered at Mount Morris, Perry, Castile, and Portageville. The Castile entrance is the most direct (and is open all year), on County Highway 38, reached by Glen Iris Road or State Road 19A, two miles south of the town of Castile.

B&B = Boxer and Breakfront

GENESEE FALLS INN
Portageville

Honors for largest breakfront in this book go to this inn, a red brick landmark that has been housing guests since 1870. The mahogany monster dominates the dining room just as surely as the portrait of John L. Sullivan, in his classic boxing pose, dominates the shellacked entryway, and the grand old pump organ dominates the second-floor lobby.

The eye-focusing, marvelous tile floor was installed during World War I, and over the years the owners have added some period pieces and floral wallpaper to the guest rooms—a favorite is No. 5 with its gigantic brass bed, calico and chintz, colorful carpeting. All the rooms in the original building have some sense of history, but the five in the twenty-year-old addition are more Scandinavian-modern in feeling. This inn is perfect as headquarters for daily excursions to the Grand Canyon of the East, Letchworth State Park with its four-hundred-foot gorge.

On the top floor there's a double-decker of a porch framed by white pillars and filled with wicker. That dining room with its boxer and breakfront has mahogany rafters and a comfortable half-Victorian, half-country Colonial ambience. The food is mostly straightforward and non-greedily priced, but the kitchen does put out a filet mignon au poivre, duckling a l'orange, crabmeat-stuffed flounder, bay scallops en casserole, and a home-made frozen chocolate-mint mousse. The house specialty is beef Strogan-off.

GENESEE FALLS INN, Route 436, Portageville, New York 14536. Telephone: (716) 493-2484. Accommodations: 12 rooms and a cottage, 10 rooms with private baths; no televisions or telephones. Rates: inexpensive. No cards. Pets not permitted. Open April through November.

Getting There: The inn is a half mile from the Portageville entrance to the Letchworth State Park, located by the bridge over the Genesee River.

WESTERN NEW YORK

CHAUTAUQUA

In the southwest corner of this state with so much to offer to so many, there's the unique phenomenon known as Chautauqua, a marvelous magnet that attracts upwards of 100,000 people a year. It's a compact cultural campus, one that owes its existence to a group of Methodist ministers who in 1874 organized a summer encampment for the edification of their Sunday school teachers.

Their modest little brainchild is today a world-famous institution, an ever-renewing intellectual and spiritual experience. It's a marvelous nine-hundred-acre mecca where families of all ages and sizes can find summer fun amid concerts and lectures, operas and ballets, non-denominational church services, workshops and art exhibits.

Sailing, water-skiing, and windsurfing on the ninety-mile-long lake; waterborne cruises on the *Chautauqua Belle* paddlewheeling passengers back into the nineteenth century; golf on the institution's own course and tennis on its courts; day camps for the very young and youth clubs for the teenagers; a youth orchestra of half a hundred high school students, a Festival Orchestra of eighty-five older students (in addition to Chautauqua's own resident symphony orchestra)—these are only some of the varied activities. There's also an opera company, dancing lessons, instruction in art and various crafts, and each morning, promptly at 10:45, a lecture. It's a sacred tradition in this quiet grove of trees with a wealth of ole-timey cottages, bicycles instead of cars, soft drinks instead of hard. Economics, estate management, foreign affairs, psychology and sociology, politics—the range of subjects presented by name speakers is endless, and there's a guaranteed debate with a good deal of audience participation.

Some nine thousand Chautauquans study music, dance, theater, and art—some of them by invitation and audition only—and there's also a healthy force of the alumnae of the famed Chautauqua Literary and Scientific Circle, an innovative home-study program that later developed into correspondence courses, book clubs, and other self-improvement programs that spread the good name of Chautauqua clear across the country.

Friday night concerts with superstars are another regular draw during the nine-week, June–August season; but there's a hardy crew of regulars who remain on campus year round, utilizing the cross-country trails, exploring the neighboring areas, resting themselves for another renewal of this one-of-a-kind culture camp.

Turn-of-the-Century Comfort
ST. ELMO HOTEL
Chautauqua

In 1894 the St. Elmo opened its doors as a quiet little inn, and over the years it has expanded as the demand for rooms grew, as more and more people discovered the delights of Chautauqua. Single and double rooms, along with suites and their cottages, have, however, kept their Victorian charm. Like the dormers, the carefully maintained red clapboard siding, the paned windows, and the main lobby with its pressed-tin ceiling and its array of wicker furniture, they are vibrant echoes from the past.

At meal times—guests are summoned by a bell—those who have spent morning and afternoon nurturing soul and mind are fed (while sitting on spindle chairs that were there in the beginning) a hearty array of basic foods. There's a choice of three entrées such as roast leg of lamb or turkey, corned beef and cabbage, baked haddock, chicken teriyaki, ribs and noodles. Breads and desserts are made on the premises.

ST. ELMO HOTEL, Vincent and Pratt avenues, Chatauqua, New York 14722. Telephone: (716) 357-2285. Accommodations: 98 rooms, 37 with private baths; some cottages and suites and family-sized apartments; no televisions or telephones. Rates: moderate to expensive; American plan, European plan, or modified American plan. No cards. Pets not permitted. Open late June through late August.

Getting There: Check into the main Chautauqua Institution gate and request a car pass for delivering luggage to the inn.

Chautauqua

A Victorian Grand Dame

ATHENAEUM HOTEL
Chautauqua

Dominating the corner of South Terrace and Janes avenues is the gloriously revitalized Grand Dame of Chautauqua, the Athenaeum, built in 1881, just seven years after those Methodist ministers gathered their first Sunday School teachers together for a summer encampment. Now gleaming and remarkably refined, this gingerbread giant with its elegant wicker-filled lobby, its high ceiling, and unbelievably spacious dining rooms—some of the staff can point out where Thomas Edison used to sit—is at the pinnacle of Chautauqua accommodations.

There are numerous guest houses, other inns and hotels, and all kinds of cottages to rent for the season; but the Athenaeum is the class act in town. Some of the rooms overlook lovely Chautauqua Lake, others are in a annex constructed in 1924; but all have been thoroughly modernized and afford the most comfortable accommodations for those who want the Chautauqua experience.

The Athenaeum, with its polite, caring corps of caretakers, its solid three-times-a-day meal service of meat and potatoes kind of fare (rates are strictly American plan), its grand old wraparound porches and super-sized sitting rooms, is the place to check into for total immersion in pampering.

ATHENAEUM HOTEL, Janes and South Terrace avenues, Chautauqua, New York 14722. Telephone: (716) 357-4444. Accommodations: 160 rooms, each with private bath; telephones but no televisions. Rates: moderate to expensive, American plan. No cards. Pets not permitted. Open from late June through late August.

Getting There: Check into the main gate of the Chautauqua Institution, on State Road 394, and get a gate ticket.

Athenaeum Hotel
Chatauqua

A Budget-Stretcher

SPENCER HOTEL
Chautauqua

Not all accommodations are as refreshingly Victorian as the Athenaeum or as expansive as the St. Elmo. Many of the hostelries in Chautauqua are rather simple affairs, and of that collection, a favorite is the Spencer, built in 1908.

It's not elaborate, the lobby is small, and the rooms do not look out on the lake. But the level of maintenance is a fussy one, the staff at the front desk is all smiles, and the rooms are fairly spacious.

Another advantage is that there's no required American plan eating. Spencer guests can live off the land, or go off campus, especially if they want some wine or something stronger with their meals.

A final point—rates are reasonable, guaranteed budget pleasers.

SPENCER HOTEL, Palestine Avenue, Chautauqua, New York 14722. Telephone: (716) 357-3785. Accommodations: 34 rooms, each with private bath; no televisions or telephones. Rates: inexpensive to low moderate. No cards. Pets not permitted. Open late June through late August.

Getting There: Check into the main gate and obtain a car pass to deliver luggage. *About 25 mi W. of Ellcottville*

An Antiquer's Paradise

WILLIAM SEWARD INN
Westfield

High on a grassy knoll near the Lake Erie Plain, which rolls gently to the hills around Lake Chautauqua, Bruce and Barbara Johnson have created an ideal country inn, one that perfectly combines a great sense of history and all the modern amenities.

The two-story mansion now transformed into an inn was built about 1821, and fifteen years later was the residence of no less a New York statesman than William Henry Seward. A young attorney from Auburn (where his later home is now a museum), Seward was an agent for the Holland Land Company, a consortium of six Dutch banks that bought thousands of acres in the area from Robert Morris, "the financier of the American Revolution," in 1792.

174

The mansion used to stand in town, near the railroad station, but in 1966 it was moved to this more majestic site, and now the Greek Revival portico looks out proudly at much of the domain that Seward commanded. From the second-floor front room, with its fine canopy four-poster and a giant armoire, and cheerful wallpaper on walls and ceiling, there's a splendid view of that domain. From the porch framed by the trio of pillars, one looks across the forest to Lake Erie; at night there's the twinkle of lights from Canada.

Below that room the Johnsons operate their antique shop. In this inn everything is for sale, everything the Johnsons collected during many months of antique-hunting in this area and in New England. Fairly priced and efficiently displayed, the antiques add much to the atmosphere, but the shop is open to the public only from 11 to 4. The Johnsons do not want to disturb inn guests at either end of their day. In the mornings the guests rally in the handsome dining room (which has its original wallpaper and china to match—the Johnsons, typically, spent months searching for exactly the right pattern) for fresh orange juice, fruit, and something special from Barbara's repertory. Her eggs Benedict are a marvel of a variation on the theme, sauced with a sour cream–cheddar cheese combination and served with a trio of sausages.

Barbara, a native of Palo Alto, California, displays other talents in this easy-to-recommend-with-enthusiasm hostelry. Her window treatments are textbook examples from a decorator with a sure eye for color and balance; her accent pieces are fantastic.

Barbara and Bruce, the latter a graduate of Denver University's Restaurant and Hotel School and experienced in the trade in both this area and the Caribbean, put their dream of an inn together quickly. They bought the old Seward mansion in December 1982 and greeted their first guest six months later.

Their inn makes the perfect headquarters for exploring the town of Westfield, whose streets are lined with fine nineteenth-century homes, sparkling examples of Federal, Greek Revival, Gothic, Italianate, and country shingle styles. A dozen of those homes are now occupied by antique shops; another, the Federal McClurg Mansion built in 1820, serves as the Chautauqua County Historical Society. Eason Hall next door is where the annual antique show is held the first weekend in August. The preceding weekend there's a lively arts and crafts festival in the town park.

Westfield is the home of Das Puppenspiel, a professional troupe of puppeteers who have a workshop on Main Street open to the public. Close by is the Greek Revival Patterson Library with an art gallery, and the headquarters of the Welch Foods corporation. Westfield is the Grape Juice Capital of the World.

Founder Charles Edgar Welch decreed that "God did not mean the grape to be fermented!" His vineyards and those of the Mogen David company and others have made this area the world's primary grower of Concord grapes. If you want your grape juice with a bit of zing, there's the Johnson Estate Winery nearby, and they give tours of their operation.

The best wine list in Westfield is at the Bark Grill at 14 East Pearl Street. That's where John and Barbara Buczek are in charge of a knockout of a menu bristling with the likes of veal loin chops in a cream-chive sauce; tournedos bordelaise; chateaubriand béarnaise; frog legs topped with shallots, mushrooms, and tomatoes; and a super blue cheese–dressed salad.

WILLIAM SEWARD INN, South Portage Road, Westfield, New York 14787. Telephone: (716) 326-4151. Accommodations: ten rooms, each with private bath; no televisions or telephones. Rates: moderate; includes full breakfast. No cards. Children under 12 not permitted; no pets. Open all year.

Getting There: The inn is 2.6 miles from the junction of U.S. 20 with State Road 394, and 5 miles from the Westfield Exit off the New York State Thruway.

160 Years Young
LELAND HOUSE
Springville

New York banker H.G. Leland was responsible for this grand old Victorian
structure, a turreted three-story that must have been the talk of the town
when it went up in 1879. Leland was building on the foundations of the old
Springville House, which greeted its first guest in 1824—that was shortly
after the name of the town was changed from Fiddler's Green.

Travelers to Leland's hotel arrived by the newly completed Springville
and Sardinia Railroad, disembarking to walk on wooden sidewalks to their
quarters. A few years later the Buffalo, Rochester and Pittsburgh Railroad
arrived in Springville, bringing more visitors, including William Jennings
Bryan and the great Jim Thorpe, who did part of his training for the Olympics on Springville streets.

The Leland House has been witness to it all: the construction of the
Civil War–period Blakeley House and Walters Pharmacy building, the 1868
Simon Brothers building and the Springville Journal–Brown Shoe Store
building. And the disastrous fires that swept across the town in 1868, again
eleven years later, then in 1894 and 1946. Because the Leland House was
spared, today the traveler can relive part of the past of a simple little settlement in western New York.

Antiques in the guest rooms were born with the hotel; they were not imported. Accommodations are functional, clean, and definitely pleasing to the budget, as are the tariffs in the ground floor dining room, which specializes in chicken and biscuits, chops, noontime salads and sandwiches, and solid breakfasts that start at 7 am for early-rising explorers.

Buffalo and Lake Erie are less than an hour away; Chautauqua, Jamestown, and Dunkirk are about as close, and in Dunkirk there's the Woodbury Vineyards on South Roberts Road. With some twenty thousand acres of grapes in the ground, Chautauqua County is the largest grape-growing area in the country outside California, and at Woodbury there's an annual mid-May Wine and Apple Blossom Festival, a champagne celebration over the July 4 holiday, and then harvest activities in September and October.

LELAND HOUSE, 26 East Main Street, Springville, New York 14141. Telephone: (716) 592-7631. Accommodations: 11 rooms sharing baths; telephones but no televisions. Rates: inexpensive. Cards: MC, V. Pets not permitted. Open all year.

Getting There: The inn is in the center of town about 35 miles south of Buffalo. *10 mi No. of Ellicottville*

A Family Success Story

BUTTERNUT INN
Chaffee

The trees out front are butternut, the sign is made of butternut, as is some of the handsomely crafted furniture inside, and I suppose before too long the Slocum clan will be serving butternut pie and ice cream. It must have occured to them—they have thought of everything else to ease their guests, both those who come for dinner and those who come to spend the night, into an innkeeper's idealization of the perfect place.

The Butternut Inn opened its doors to the public in July 1982. Keith and Arletta Slocum are at the head of the family that transformed a 1930 farmhouse into a dream of delight; son Ken is in charge of the kitchen, and lives in an attic apartment above the guest rooms; daughter Denise works as waitress and contributed the samplers on bedroom walls; son Eric buses the tables. An earlier generation even got into the act: Arletta's father, Wilbur W. Smith, has several pen and ink drawings on display.

Chef Kenny's artistry is on display nightly—salmon patties with lemon sauce, chicken laden with a ham-apricot stuffing, tarragon lamb chops which he marinates in an oil-vinegar-garlic bath before committing them to the flames; homemade soups, breads, and muffins, and steak Edward enhanced with just the right amount of garlic and chopped onions swimming in burgundy.

Arletta the omnipresent puts in her fair share of kitchen time before donning the robes and smiles of inn hostess. Her salad dressing, made from fresh basil plucked from the side-of-the-inn herb garden, is superb, and she should probably be given credit for Grandma's rice pudding if not for the Linzertorte, the peanut butter pie, the chocolate-date-nut cake, and other concoctions.

In vintage country inn style, the changed-nightly menu is posted near the entrance, and there's seldom an empty chair among the forty-six in the pair of dining rooms and on a porch that redefines the word cheerful. It's a strawberry burst of joy with calico cloths and curtains, an ideal place for the full-scale breakfasts that come streaming out of the back room: eggs, buttermilk pancakes, fresh fruits, good coffee. In the slower months of the year, silver-tray Continental breakfasts are provided overnight guests, but at all times, travelers fortunate enough to find this gem are greeted with fresh fruit, cheese and crackers, an ice bucket and wine (from a very select, excellent wine list), and generous doses of honest hospitality.

The most recent addition to this happy little domain is the downstairs lounge, furnished with the kind of conversation-stopping antiques found in the guest rooms: buggy seats serving as couches, an old ironing board transformed into a cocktail table. A set of checkers, a television, and some reading material are there for inn guests, those over-nighting and those waiting for their turn at the Slocums' table of treats.

There are other antiques two miles south of the inn in the town of Arcade, where the Arcade and Attica Railroad chugs its way across the countryside from Decoration Day through October. Among the rolling stock is the "Warwick," the 1886 private railroad car which President Grover Cleveland used on his wedding trip. In business since 1881, the railroad is still a freight hauler, and for ninety minutes takes today's passengers back into the era of steam.

BUTTERNUT INN, Route 16 and Genesee Road, Chaffee, New York 14030. Telephone: (716) 496-8987. Accommodations: three rooms, each with private bath; no televisions or telephones. Rates: moderate; includes breakfast. Cards: MC, V. Pets not permitted. Closed January 1.

Getting There: The inn is on State Road 16 at the intersection with Genesee Road a mile south of the town of Chaffee.

About 20 mi. S. of Buffalo
" 15 mi. N. of Ellicottville

see Fannie's tape

A Campus of Craftsmen
ROYCROFT INN
East Aurora

The spirit of Elbert Hubbard not only survives in his beloved Roycroft Campus, it thrives. The man who wrote "A Message to Garcia" almost seems alive today as one walks among the solidly built stone structures, browses in the gift shops, picks over antiques and artifacts, watches craftsmen at work.

In the manner of England's William Morris, Elbert Hubbard, a successful soap company executive and publicist *extraordinaire* possessing a magic way with words, founded in the 1890s the Roycroft Shop. Named after seventeenth-century printer Thomas Roycroft, the shop soon grew into an entire complex of kindred spirits, gathered to expound Hubbard's philosophy: "I believe in the hands that work; in the brains that think; in the hearts that love."

Furniture and wrought iron were produced by the Roycrofters, and individual schools of music, sculpture, and painting were established, along with an active printing press. Roycroft Printers, regarded by the founder as the most important of the several industries and endeavors he fostered, produced beautiful hand-bound books along with his "magazine of protest," *The Philistine*, and a more ambitious effort called *The Fra* (Hubbard was known to friends and fans as Fra Elbertus or the Fra).

Fannie lived next door

The first printing shop, a small one-room structure next to Hubbard's home, patterned after Wordsworth's church in Grasmere, England, was gradually enlarged until in 1903 it was turned into the Roycroft Inn. Under the tutelage of the Turgeons, restaurant entrepreneurs elsewhere in the state, today it's home for the solid kind of fare the Turgeons produce so well—onion soup, prime rib, Australian lobster tails, sirloins, king crab, chicken with an orange-whiskey sauce—in a dining room alive with the workmanship of the original Roycrofters.

Upstairs are the guest rooms, furnished in a style befitting the followers of John Ruskin and William Morris. Room A is newly revitalized and has a kitchenette complete with a set of Roycroft china patterned after the original, a spacious bathroom, twin beds and some stenciling. Room F has a bird's-eye maple bed made on campus, and G a spacious sitting room.

The inn also has an "As You Like It" English pub and large public rooms, and just outside are all the solid reminders of Hubbard's dream. There's the 1899 stone Gothic chapel, one-time meeting hall for the Roycrofters, now the Town Hall and Museum, maintained by the Aurora Historical Society. Memorabilia from Hubbard's heyday are on display as they are at the Elbert Hubbard Library Museum.

180

The Roycroft Campus Gift Shop is housed in the former Blacksmith Shop which once produced all kinds of bronze, copper, and silver accessory pieces; the Roycroft Power Plant (Hubbard believed in self-sufficiency) now is home to an antiques dealer, an art gallery, a pottery studio, a jeweler, and the East Aurora Chamber of Commerce.

Elbert Hubbard went down at sea—aboard the *Lusitania*—but he lives again in his Roycroft Inn and among the modern-day Roycroft artisans, who believe the words of Fra Elbertus: "Failure is only for those who think failure."

ROYCROFT INN, 40 South Grove Street, East Aurora, New York 14052. Telephone: (716) 652-9030. Accommodations: 16 rooms, some with kitchenettes, some suites, some that share baths; no televisions or telephones. Rates: inexpensive to moderate; includes Continental breakfast. Cards: AE, MC, V. Pets not permitted. Open all year.

Getting There: East Aurora is a suburb of Buffalo, and Grove Street is 1.5 miles from the East Aurora exit of Highway 400; turn left at the ivy-covered Gothic Town Hall. The inn is the third building on the left.

A Quintessential Country Inn

ASA RANSOM HOUSE
Clarence Hollow

Here is an inn that is picture-postcard perfect, from its sweeping expanse of green lawn behind an eggshell-white picket fence, to its ivy-covered weathered brick, with red shutters, beautifully manicured gardens, and cheerful front porch—precisely the appearance, the setting, the spirit most of us hope to find in a country inn.

The spell is sustained inside—by the friendly greetings of the long-gowned staff, by the extremely high level of maintenance, by the character of the public and private rooms, the great sense of taste in the decor, the stewardship of an important part of the area's past.

Asa Ransom was a silversmith who in 1799 accepted the offer of the Holland Land Company to "build and operate a tavern" on acreage in the "hollow of the ledge" near a pine grove. His simple log cabin served as both home and hostelry, and in 1801, alongside the creek which bears his name today, he built a sawmill and, two years later, a gristmill, the ruins of which have been found at the back end of the inn property. The tavern he built in the 1850s forms the core of the present-day inn. The brick wall in the entry

181

Asa Ransom House

hall was the outside of his building and the Tap Room with its oil lights part of his tavern. Today it's a wonderfully evocative setting.

There are similar strong vibrations in the pair of dining rooms, one rather formal with Windsor chairs and garden views for non-smokers, and one a mite more rustic, for smokers. Such distinctions are typical of the Asa Ransom Inn. So are the freshly baked breads, the veal kissed ever so gently with Madeira, the simmering soups spooned out of the kettle, and the unusual corned beef, locally smoked and served with a fine apple-raisin sauce.

The library has an assortment of games, books, and periodicals, and there's a small, select gift shop along with a quartet of rooms which are as gracefully furnished as everything else in this quintessential country inn. The Green Room is almost suite-sized, with a pair of double beds and a fine view of the herb garden. Gold has stenciling, part of the building's original brick wall, twin brass beds; Blue has a canopy bed; and the Red Room with its 1825 cannonball double bed looks out at that expanse of lawn with its picket fence.

ASA RANSOM HOUSE, 10529 Main Street, Clarence Hollow, New York 14031. Telephone: (416) 759-2315. Accommodations: four rooms, each with private bath; no televisions or telephones. Rates: moderate; includes full breakfast. No cards. Pets not permitted. Open all year.

Getting There: The inn is 12 miles from Exit 48A of the New York Thruway; take State Road 77 a few hundred meters to State Road 5 and turn right onto Main Street; the inn is across the street from the post office.

Across the River and onto the Lake
OBAN INN
Niagara-on-the-Lake

No, it's not in New York; but the inn is so special, the town so magnificent, and the short drive from Niagara Falls so spectacular that the Oban simply *must* be in this book.

First, the drive: leaving the drama of the falls, the Niagara Parkway rolls gently along, past fine homes and well-maintained farms, many of which sell their freshly picked produce in roadside stands. Near the immaculate town of Niagara-on-the-Lake there's Fort George, built by the British as a defensive bulwark to replace Fort Niagara across the river—after the American Revolution they had to surrender that fort. Fort George, captured by the Americans during the War of 1812, then recaptured by the

183

British, was carefully restored in the 1930s. Today it serves as the focal point of the Canadian Parks' interpretation program, with uniformed guides reenacting nineteenth-century infantry and artillery drills, explaining the lifestyle of troopers at the time of the War of 1812.

Second, the town: in sum, it's a gem. Swept streets, scrubbed houses, manicured gardens create an overwhelming sense of British order and propriety. The quiet, tree-lined streets are ideal for strolling, and the main shopping streets are filled with temptations. Start your tour at the Niagara Historical Society Museum, on Castlereagh Street between King and Wellington, by picking up brochures and a map for self-guided walks.

Finally, the inn: it, too, is a gem, one that sparkles with elegance. Its dining rooms go on forever, and they feed thousands, especially during the summer season; their guest rooms are handsomely furnished, and some overlook the lake; there's a piano bar and a warm, inviting retreat named Shaw's Corner. A fine oil portrait of George Bernard Shaw hangs over the cheery fireplace, and on other walls are photos of the stars of past and present Shaw Festivals, an annual May-October happening (since 1961) built around the plays of Shaw as well as those of Noel Coward, Ben Travers, and Edmond Rostand.

The three-story inn was originally built as a grand Colonial home by Duncan Milloy, a prosperous lake captain from Oban, Scotland. Completed in the 1820s, it's one of the oldest survivors in the town, and while it has housed guests for most of its years, it was not until the Burroughs family took over in 1963 that the inn, completely restored and revitalized, reached its present zenith.

Dining rooms, a porch, and a glassed-in patio overlook the beautifully manicured landscaping leading gently to the shores of Lake Ontario. There are more blooms inside: the Oban Inn makes highly dramatic use of floral arrangements.

Across the Niagara River from inn and town is the American village of Youngstown, the counterpart of Niagara-on-the-Lake, more American Colonial than British Victorian in style. It, too, has an interesting inventory of ancient and honorable homes, and it, too, has a fort—Old Fort Niagara, boasting the oldest building in the Great Lakes area, the French Castle, constructed in 1726. There are regularly scheduled military reenactments, mock battles, grand reviews, fife and drum performances, occasional craft demonstrations—all carried out by authentically garbed participants.

A few miles to the south the city of Lewiston, seven miles north of Niagara Falls, has its own kind of sleepy, historic charm, much of it dating from the rebuilding of the town afer the British razed it during the War of 1812. Lewiston is supposedly the site of the world's first cocktail: the proprietor of a Center Street tavern, Catherine Hustler (itself a name of note) added the tail feather of a stuffed cock pheasant to a blend of gin and herbed wine before serving.

At the end of Lewiston is a two-hundred-acre state park carved alongside the Niagara River Gorge, and at its center is Artpark, a picnic place *extraordinaire* surrounding a twenty-four-hundred-seat theater with an outdoor arena and big-name performers, ballet companies, musicals.

A different kind of performance is given at Power Vista on Lewiston Road, located 350 feet above the Niagara River Gorge. Graphic displays and theaters tell the story of the Niagara Power Project, all 2,400,000 kilowatts of it. There's a grand Thomas Hart Benton mural of the famous Father Hennepin standing at the falls in 1678.

Close by is the Fatima Shrine, a domed basilica surrounded by life-sized statues and crowned by a thirteen-foot, ten-ton representation of Our Lady of Fatima. The Barnabite Fathers are responsible for this place of prayer, and there are regularly scheduled masses as well as special observances, including Mary's Day on the first Sunday of May and the Coronation Feast on the second Sunday of August.

OBAN INN, Gate Street (P.O. Box 94), Niagara-on-the-Lake, Ontario LOS 1JO, Canada. Telephone: (416) 468-2165. Accommodations: 23 rooms, each with private bath, television; 20 rooms in the main building, three in Oban House adjoining the inn and used as a conference center. Rates: moderate. Cards: AE, MC, V. Well-behaved pets permitted. Open all year.

Getting There: Niagara-on-the-Lake is a dozen miles north of Niagara Falls, and the inn is on the corner of Gate and Front streets, fronting Lake Ontario.

INDEX

CHILDREN WELCOME

Please see listings for individual inns for age restrictions pertaining to children.

PETS ACCEPTED

Please see listings for individual inns for any restrictions pertaining to pets.

INNS WITH SWIMMING POOLS

Auberge Des 4 Saisons, Shandaken, 68–69
Copper Hood Inn, Allaben, 68
Gideon Putnam, Saratoga Springs, 84–86
Greenville, Arms, Greenville, 76–78
Shandaken Inn, Shandaken, 70
Shepherd's Neck Inn, Montauk Point, 17–18
Southampton Inn, Southampton, 7–8
Swiss Hutte, Hillsdale, 53–54
Townsend Manor Inn, Greenport, 25–27
Troutbeck, Amenia, 49–50
Village Latch Inn, Southampton, 8–9
Winter Clove Inn, Round Top, 75–76

INNS WITH RESTAURANTS

Adelphia Putnam, Saratoga Springs, 86–87
Algonquin, New York City, 29–30
American Stanhope, New York City, 30–31
Asa Ransom House, Clarence Hollow, 181–183
Auberge Des 4 Saisons, Shandaken, 68–69
Aurora Inn, Aurora, 153–154
Balsam House, Chestertown, 96–97
Bark Eater, Keene, 113–114
Beekman Arms, Rhinebeck, 50–51
Benn Conger Inn, Groton, 151–152
Bird & Bottle Inn, Garrison, 39–40
Box Tree, Purdy, 34–38
Brae Loch Inn, Cazenovia, 129–131
Brick House Inn, Eaton, 126
Butternut Inn, Chaffee, 178–179
Chequit Inn, Shelter Island, 20–21
Clinton House, Clinton, 128
Colgate Inn, Hamilton, 124–125
Country Road Lodge, Warrensburg, 94–95
Depuy Canal House, High Falls, 65–66

Garnet Hill Lodge, North River, 99–100
Geneva on the Lake, Geneva, 160–161
Gideon Putnam, Saratoga Springs, 84–86
Glen Iris Inn, Castile, 166–168
Golden Eagle Inn, Garrison's Landing, 40–42
Green Mountain View Inn, Tannersville, 71
Greenville Arms, Greenville, 76–78
Hedges House, East Hampton, 10–11
Hedges on Blue Mountain Lake, Blue Mountain Lake, 104–105
Hemlock Hall, Blue Mountain Lake, 105–106
Hewitt's Ruschmeyer's Inn, Montauk, 17
Horned Dorset Inn, Leonardsville, 122–123
Hudson House, Cold Spring, 43–44
Hulbert House, Boonville, 134–135
Huntting Inn, East Hampton, 11–12
Inn at Quogue, Quogue, 3–5
Inn at Shaker Mill Farm, Canaan, 54–56
Kittle House, Mount Kisco, 35–37
L'Hostellerie Bressane, Hillsdale, 51–53
Leland House, Springville, 177–178
Lincklaen House, Cazenovia, 131–132
Maidstone Arms, East Hampton, 12–13
Merrill Magee House, Warrensburg, 92–94
Millhof Inn, Stephentown, 56–58
Mirror Lake Inn, Lake Placid, 110–111
No. 1022, New York City, 32
Oban Inn, Niagara-on-the-Lake, Ontario, 183–185
Otesaga Hotel, Cooperstown, 120–121
Peconic Lodge, Shelter Island Heights, 24–25
Ram's Head Inn, Shelter Island, 23–24
Redcoat's Return, Elka Park, 73–74
Roycroft Inn, East Aurora, 180–181
1770 House, East Hampton, 13–15
Shandaken Inn, Shandaken, 70
Shepherd's Neck Inn, Montauk Point, 17–18

191

COUNTRY INNS GUIDEBOOKS
In 101 Productions' Series

Country Inns of the Far West: California $7.95
Country Inns of the Far West: Pacific Northwest $7.95
Country Inns of New England $7.95
Country Inns of New York State $7.95
Country Inns of the Mid-Atlantic $7.95
Country Inns of the Old South $7.95
Country Inns of the Great Lakes $4.95
Country Inns Cookery $6.95

If you cannot find these books in your local bookstore,
they may be ordered from the publisher:
101 Productions, 834 Mission Street, San Francisco CA 94103
Please add $1.00 per copy for postage and handling.
California residents add sales tax.

TO ORDER: Indicate quantity for each title above and fill in form below.
Send with check or money order to 101 Productions.

NAME _____

ADDRESS _____ __

CITY_____ STATE_____ ZIP_____

BIOGRAPHICAL NOTES

ROBERT W. TOLF
A dean of Southern restaurant critics and an internationally known writer whose books and articles have been translated into Spanish, German, and Swedish, Robert W. Tolf is a tireless traveler and a prolific author. Since settling in Florida in 1971 after a distinguished career in the Foreign Service, living in Scandinavia and Switzerland, Tolf has averaged two books a year, including the most recent *Discover Florida: A Guide to the Unique Sites and Sights* (Manatee); *Addison Mizner: Architect to the Affluent* (Gale Graphics); *Florida Restaurant Guide*, Tampa Bay and Gold Coast editions (Buchan Publications); and a revised, greatly expanded edition of *Country Inns of the Old South* (101 Productions). A graduate of Harvard with a Ph.D. from the University of Rochester, Tolf is an editor of *Florida Trend* magazine, and his restaurant reviews, travel and "Good Life" columns appear regularly in the *Fort Lauderdale News/Sun-Sentinel*. A former Senior Research Fellow of the Hoover Institution on War, Revolution and Peace, Tolf is also the author of *The Russian Rockefellers: The Saga of the Nobel Family and the Russian Oil Industry*, which won a Thomas Newcomen award in 1980 as one of the best three books on business history published in this country during the preceding three years.

ROXANE S. RAUCH
Roxane S. Rauch is a native New Yorker, a multi-talented woman whose credits include twenty years of promotional experience in New York City's and New York State's two largest industries—fashion and tourism. She was administrator of New York City's apparel manufacturing association (Fashion Capital of the World), and an executive with the New York Convention and Visitors' Bureau. Her experience in retailing, advertising, and public relations; running her own lecture bureau, collecting vintage show clothes, and writing shopping columns for *New Florida* magazine and other publications have given her a strong sense of the reality of today as well as the magic of nostalgia. In *Country Inns of New York State*, she returns home to give testimony to her life-long love affair with her native New York.

ROY KILLEEN
Roy Killeen, who created the full-page drawings for this book, is an architect, formerly with Anshen and Allen of San Francisco. He has also designed 101 Productions' "Mini-Mansion" series of historical architectural models and illustrated most of the other books in the Country Inns series, as well as a number of other 101 books.